MOSES MAIM

C000256605

ARABIC THOUGHT AND CULTURE

This new series is designed to provide straightforward introductions for the western reader to some of the major figures and movements of Arabic thought. Philosophers, historians, and geographers are all seminal figures in the history of thought, and some names, such as Averroes and Avicenna, are already part of the western tradition. Mathematicians, linguistic theorists and astronomers have as significant a part to play as groups of thinkers such as the Illuminationists. With the growing importance of the Arab world on the international scene, these succinct and authoritative works will be welcomed not only by teachers and students of Arab history and of philosophy, but by journalists, travellers, teachers of EFL and businessmen – in fact any who have to come to an understanding of this non-western culture in the course of their daily work.

The brief of each author is to take stock of the state of each of the fields covered, to expound the main controversies, and to include an annotated bibliographic guide for further study.

Also available in this series

THE ARABIC LINGUISTIC TRADITION
Georges Bohas, Jean-Patrick Guillaume, Djamel Eddine Kouloughli

IBN KHALDŪN
Aziz Al-Azmeh

MOSES MAIMONIDES

OLIVER LEAMAN

ROUTLEDGE
LONDON AND NEW YORK

First published 1990
by Routledge
11 New Fetter Lane, London EC4P 4EE

Simultaneously published in the USA and Canada
by Routledge
a division of Routledge, Chapman and Hall, Inc.
29 West 35th Street, New York, NY 10001

© 1990 Oliver Leaman

Printed in Great Britain by T. J. Press (Padstow) Ltd,
Padstow, Cornwall

Phototypeset by Input Typesetting Ltd, London

All rights reserved. No part of this book may be reprinted or reproduced
or utilized in any form or by an electronic, mechanical, or other means,
now known or hereafter invented, including photocopying and recording,
or in any information storage or retrieval system, without permission in
writing from the publishers.

British Library Cataloguing in Publication Data

Leaman, Oliver
Moses Maimonides.
1. Jewish philosophy. Maimonides
I. Title
181'.06'0924

ISBN 0–415–03481–7

Library of Congress Cataloging in publication Data

Leaman, Oliver.
Moses Maimonides/Oliver Leaman.
p.   cm.
Bibliography: p.
Includes index.
ISBN 0–415–03481–7.–ISBN 0–415–03608–9 (pbk.)
1. Maimonides, Moses, 1135–1204–Contributions in philosophy.
2. Philosophy, Jewish. 3. Philosophy, Medieval. I. Title.
B759.M34L37 1989
181'.06–dc20   89–10444

For Rosa, Imogen, and Perdita

Contents

Preface

There are many books and articles which deal with aspects of Maimonides and his thought, and any author requires a good reason for adding to what already exists. In this book I argue that there is a need for a re-examination of the traditional interpretation of the philosophical thought of Moses Maimonides. That interpretation is based upon two principles, both of which are suspect. The first principle is that Maimonides set about a strategy of hiding his real opinions beneath a disguise of careful and conflicting language, which alerted his supporters to his genuine views while pacifying the suspicions of those incapable of understanding or appreciating his real message. It will come as no surprise to those who have come across some of my work in the area of medieval philosophy that I oppose this approach to Maimonides. Such a process of interpretation falls neatly within the orientalist mode of analysis, which continually looks for a hidden and more significant meaning beneath the text itself, based as it is upon a subtle rejection of the value of the text as a philosophical argument. On the contrary, I argue here that Maimonides presents powerful and intriguing arguments which deserve serious philosophical consideration, raising as they do issues concerning the appropriate analysis of language and the notion of a human point of view. It is a great shame that the extreme care which Maimonides took over his means of presentation has been distorted by the orientalists to represent a linguistic device to disguise his argument, whereas in reality he was trying to present the argument in as clear and terse a form as possible. One of the results of the influence of the traditional interpretation of Maimonides is the proliferation of extraordinarily 'scholarly' articles on his work, with a text almost submerged under footnotes and respectful references to other commentators. Although there is interesting material in much of this work, it often succeeds in treating as a sideline the actual argument which Maimonides produces. In this book the emphasis throughout is upon the arguments themselves.

The second principle which will be challenged here is that Maimonides is a specifically Jewish thinker. The majority of the literature dealing with his thought tries to relate his philosophical and legal work, with the emphasis upon the reconciliation of Aristotelian philosophy and Jewish religious principles. This is an interesting topic, and was obviously of concern to Maimonides, but it is a great error to see his philosophical ambitions as being limited to this issue. Maimonides was Jewish, and a leader of his community both while alive and even today through his persisting thoughts as represented in his work. Judaism was the context within which he worked, but of far more importance when we come to his philosophy is the influence of the tradition of philosophy in the Islamic world. In this book he is treated as a member of the distinguished group of thinkers in the Islamic world who took on board the methodology of Aristotle and applied it to difficult conceptual issues in interesting and perceptive ways. The main focus is on his *Guide of the Perplexed* and some of the main philosophical concerns he has in that work. There is no attempt here at providing a comprehensive guide to Maimonides' philosophical thought, but something of the flavour of his approach to important philosophical issues. Philosophy is a pursuit with universal aspirations (hence the opposition by particular religious institutions) and it is misleading to think of Maimonides as a specifically *Jewish* philosopher. On the other hand, when we consider the breadth and depth of his work we are at the same time celebrating the richness of the cultural milieu which the Islamic world constituted at that period of history.

Many people and institutions have helped me with this book. Libraries in a variety of places have been of great assistance, as has my college library. The British Academy kindly assisted financially some of my work on Maimonides' use of the notion of imagination. A version of the chapter on imagination appears in *Religion* (1988) 18, pp. 69–80, and was presented as a paper at the University of Cambridge 850th Anniversary Maimonides Lecture Series in 1985. I have presented part of the book as papers on a number of occasions at the Universities of Exeter, Liverpool and Wales, and am grateful for the comments by participants. Dr Erwin Rosenthal has yet again proved to be immensely stimulating during the course of our discussions on Maimonides, and I am profoundly grateful to him. I have enjoyed and learnt a good deal from the discussions I have had with Peter Edwards on more general philosophical topics. My thanks go to them both. They are in no way responsible for any errors which exist in the text.

Liverpool,
June 1988   O. N. H. L.

Abbreviations

A — *Averroes and his Philosophy*, O. Leaman (Oxford University Press, Oxford, 1988).

GP — *The Guide of the Perplexed*, translated and with an introduction and notes by S. Pines (University of Chicago Press, Chicago, 1963). References are in this order – book, chapter; page number.

I — *An Introduction to Medieval Islamic Philosophy*, O. Leaman (Cambridge University Press, Cambridge, 1985).

Int — 'Translator's Introduction', S. Pines, in *GP* lvii–cxxxiv.

TT — *Tahāfut al-tahāfut*, ed. M. Bouyges (Bibliotheca Arabica Scholasticorum, Série Arabe, 3; Imprimerie Catholique, Beirut, 1930); page-references are to this edition and all translations are from Averroes' *Tahāfut al-tahāfut (The Incoherence of the Incoherence)* trans. and int. S. Van Den Bergh (2 vols; Luzac, London, 1954; repr. 1969 and 1978) and incorporating the *Tahāfut al-falāsifa (The Incoherence of the Philosophers)*, al-Ghazali.

Translations are taken from the works referred to in the text, with occasional modifications.

1

The cultural background

It is the thesis of this book that Moses Maimonides falls squarely within the tradition of philosophy as it developed in the Islamic world during the period labelled medieval in the West. This sort of philosophy is frequently called Islamic philosophy, since it grew and flourished in the Islamic cultural world, but many of its protagonists were not Muslims. Jews and Christians were on occasion enthusiastic participants in the leading philosophical disputes of the time. It is not surprising that this should be the case, since this sort of philosophy is based upon the universalism of Greek thought represented at the highest level by Plato and Aristotle. They dealt with ideas and arguments which clearly originated within the Greek cultural milieu, yet equally clearly possess a far wider relevance and interest. Many of their works came to be translated into Arabic, often via Syriac, in 'Abbāsid Bagdad, along with a great mass of lesser material by commentators seeking to explain the arguments of the main Greek philosophers, and in particular Aristotle. The development of Greek thought in the Islamic world was also mediated through the neo-Platonic interpretations of Plotinus and Proclus. Greek philosophy in the Islamic world, suggestively translated by the term *falsafa* to emphasize its Greek origins, was frequently the object of controversy and persecution. It seemed to some to contravene the main principles of religion and to import a whole corpus of techniques and terminology which stood in opposition to the traditional Islamic sciences of grammar, law, theology and literature. On occasion *falsafa* was opposed by xenophobic influences in the Islamic world, suspicious of foreign influence and dubious about the need for any assistance from an ultimately non-Muslim source for conceptual problems which might arise.

Despite these problems, many outstanding thinkers arose within the Islamic world, ranging from Fārābī, Avicenna (ibn Sīnā) and Ghazālī in the East to ibn Ṭufayl, ibn Bājja and ibn Rushd in the West. There is no space here to describe the work of these thinkers directly, although it will emerge indirectly in our account of Maimonides (and for more detail on these thinkers see *I* and *A passim*). What made the thought of these philosophers so compelling to a large number of intellectuals at that time? It was the great strength of conceptual thought which they represented, and the apparently impregnable conclusions which they drew on issues of such significance as the origin of the world, the nature of human happiness, the life to come, the nature of God and the ordinary world. Many of these conclusions ran counter to the way in which Islam represented basic religious truths. The philosophers (*falāsifa*) did not conclude from this contrast that philosophy was superior to religion, or that the latter must be revised to take account of the discoveries made by the former. They tended to argue that religion presents in a simple and unsophisticated form the same sort of truth presented by philosophy, which only a few thinkers are of appropriate stature to appreciate.

There has been a great deal of argument as to whether they were really sincere in their adherence to religion, or only mouthing platitudes to save themselves from the ire of the political and religious authorities. They took to heart the tragic end of Socrates, who openly appeared to contradict the practices and beliefs of religion in Greece, and who suffered the ultimate penalty as a result of expressing himself so clearly and publicly. Such a response might seem timorous and unworthy, and it can be represented in a more favourable light by suggesting that the *falāsifa* were concerned that ordinary believers would find their faith challenged by an unsuccessful attempt at understanding the difficult conceptual points which the philosophers made about their common religion. Socrates could take a rather contemptuous attitude towards ordinary Athenians, but the *falāsifa* could not adopt a similar posture with respect to the ordinary but pious Muslims in their community. As Muslims themselves they appreciated the links which existed between their sophisticated analysis of Islam and the simple faith of their co-religionists. The *falāsifa* were obliged out of more than just self-interest, then, to preserve the simple faith of the community while initiating debate on conceptual issues among those capable of understanding and benefitting from that debate.

The rather awkward position in which the *falāsifa* found themselves vis-à-vis their local communities led them to express themselves very carefully. They did not want readers to concentrate upon those aspects of their work which seem to embody heretical or challenging doctrines if those readers were unable to understand how such doctrines are really acceptable from a religious point of view. There is no doubt that the *falāsifa* thought long and hard about how they were going to present their views, and they were concerned to portray themselves as perfectly ordinary believers with orthodox views. It is worth mentioning at this stage that there is a tradition in Islam of *taqīya*, of dissimulation of one's real view under a veil of orthodoxy to prevent the authorities from persecuting one's genuine heterodox opinions. This was particularly prevalent among Shi'ite minorities ruled by Sunni governments, and it gave rise to a well-developed tradition of esoteric (*bāṭin*) as opposed to exoteric (*ẓāhir*) writing. When one understands the tradition one is able to understand the points which the writer is really making, whereas the more naïve reader will fail to grasp these points (fortunately for the writer) and will be satisfied with the views which the writer appears to present as his own. Much of the work which has taken place on *falsafa* has assumed that much philosophical writing within this genre falls within the esoteric tradition, and to understand it one must always be alert to the constraints under which the author worked and the sort of audience which he hoped to attract as compared with the sort of audience which he hoped to placate.

I have in the past criticized the implications which the interpreters of *falsafa* have drawn from the existence of an esoteric tradition in Islam. I have argued that this approach places far too much emphasis upon the style in which the *falāsifa* wrote and not nearly enough emphasis upon their actual arguments (*I*, pp. 182–201). It leads to the analysis of philosophical works as being on a par with literary works, to an over-concentration upon minor aspects of the style as opposed to major details of the argument. It refuses to acknowledge the philosophical interest which lies within so much Islamic philosophy, and treats it as something else, something less demanding. The reason why this standard approach to Islamic philosophy is so prevalent is not difficult to discover. Most scholars in the field are primarily linguists and historians, not philosophers, and they find it much more attractive to deal with texts in terms of their linguistic and historical context as compared with their philosophical implications. Along with this goes the very different way in which Islamic philosophy is treated as compared, for example, with English philosophy or phenomenological philosophy. Islamic philosophy, in the way in which the term is used here, is the philosophy which arose in the Islamic world during the Middle Ages, just as English philosophy is the philosophy which takes place in England and phenomenology the philosophy which continues the work of Husserl and Heidegger. Modern, medieval and ancient philosophy is treated as philosophy in its own right, with a history, interesting arguments, and major figures in their own right. Islamic philosophy, though, has fallen foul of the orientalist obsession with refusing to acknowledge that people in the Islamic world actually say what they mean when they talk and write. The orientalist turn in the interpretation of Islamic philosophy has led to the development of a pseudo-subject, a literary analysis whereby one can arrive at some glimmerings of the personal opinions of the authors beneath the covering of their writings.

One might think that if any case can be made out for treating philosophy as an esoteric kind of writing, it could be made out for the sort of philosophy produced by Maimonides. Not only might it be thought that his radical questioning would set him outside his community, but the political conditions in which much of Jewry existed made dissimulation and conversion vital if existence was to be preserved. Moses ben Maimon was born between 1135 and 1138 in Córdoba, where his father was a rabbi and judge in the Jewish community. The Jewish community in Spain was well established, and on the whole thoroughly integrated into Andalusian culture. During Muslim rule there were long periods during which both Jews and Christians were tolerated and allowed to rise to high positions in the state. In cultural terms there is no doubt that the Jewish community became enthusiastic Arabic speakers and writers, and studied in depth many of the leading works produced in the Islamic scholarly world. It was quite possible for someone to remain faithful to his own religious traditions and yet at the same time try to assimilate the exciting discoveries in medicine, mathematics, astronomy, philosophy, and political thought which appeared in Arabic and largely through the work of Muslim intellectuals. Spain, *al-Andalūs*, was a repository of considerable intellectual effort, with skilfully constructed libraries, observatories, and circles of scholars quite consciously setting themselves up in opposition to the traditional fount of both Islam and early Islamic theoretical thought in the east of the empire. This opposition was not in terms of opposition to the principles of Islam, but rather an assertion of the specific climatic, intellectual, and political virtues of the West (*al-faḍā'il al-Andalus*). In philosophy, in particular, some of the most interesting work to be done occurred in Andalus, with the three major Muslim figures of ibn Ṭufayl, ibn Bajja, and the greatest of them all, ibn Rushd (Averroes).

This cultural flourishing did not run smoothly, however, and the political and military implications of living on the frontier frequently led to the invasion of Andalus from North Africa and the imposition of more fundamentalist régimes highly suspicious of both religious minorities and the complexities produced by philosophers and theologians. Unfortunately for Maimonides, the successful invasion of Córdoba by the Almohads, just one such régime, meant that there was no longer a place there for Jews living openly, and his family wandered for a while around Andalus between 1148 and 1160 before settling in Fez. It is possible that his family converted to Islam while in Fez; there is no doubt that a great many Jewish families took the opportunity to convert and preserve their lives and positions, while at the same time secretly practising their religion. At the same time it can hardly have been a secret to the authorities in what was after all the capital of the Almohad empire that people like Maimonides were diligently studying and writing on issues in Jewish law and theology, doubtless in association with other like-minded individuals. Around 1165 Maimonides and his family left Morocco and moved into Palestine, where they only stayed for six months or so, before travelling to Egypt. They took up residence in Fustat, near Cairo, and in social terms the family prospered in the more friendly environment provided by Fatimid government. The friendliness of the environment did not change with the downfall of the Fatimids brought about by Salāḥ al-din (Saladin) in 1171, and Maimonides rose to become one of the main physicians of the ruler's vizier in 1185. He attained a considerable political influence in the Jewish community world-wide, based partly on his position as 'chief rabbi' of Egypt and his eminent legal and theological reputation. Since his death his reputation in the Jewish community has if anything become even more formidable, and his works are as eagerly consulted today as they were eight hundred years ago.

His significance to the Jewish community rests largely upon the breadth of his work on law. His *Mishneh Torah* represents a complete systematization of the Oral Law, and his other works on Jewish law were attempts at bringing some sort of order and brevity into the vast amount of detail, argument, and opinions which confronted a member of the community seeking an answer to a practical or theoretical query. It is worth pointing out that this contribution by Maimonides was so distinct, and aroused so much opposition, because of its use of Islamic models in its construction of a *fiqh* (jurisprudence). As opposed to the rather chaotic mixture of Talmudic commentary and biblical exegesis which had previously existed, Maimonides sought to impose a unified and definitive view based upon his understanding of the main theological and philosophical issues. This is very much part of the Islamic tradition followed by the different legal schools, and had previously been anathema in the Jewish community, which valued the activity of sifting through varying interpretations in the texts before achieving a tentative answer. With his great codification and organization of the law Maimonides had tried to close the door on *ijtihād* (innovation) within the context of Jewish law. It is hardly surprising, then, that this attempt should have come up against so much hostility among sections of the rabbinate and legal authorities in the Jewish world. They adopted the clever strategy of attacking him not so much on account of the codification (which became immediately popular due to its vast intellectual grasp of so many disparate items) but because of his supposed denial of the possibility of resurrection and the immortality of the life to come. He wrote a separate treatise, which we shall discuss, in which he tried to escape from this charge.

The suspicion that Maimonides really had opinions which were very different from his professed opinions in his main legal works is founded upon his outstanding contribution to philosophy, the *Guide of the Perplexed (Dalālat ḥa'irīn)*, which he wrote in 1197. This is a most unusual text. Most of my discussion will be based upon the *Guide* in combination with some of the small philosophical treatises which he also wrote. Before we start that discussion it is important to state quite clearly the theoretical standpoint which is to be adopted. Most discussion of the *Guide* follows the interpretation offered by Leo Strauss and his many disciples in that it assumes that Maimonides has carefully constructed the book to ward off the naïve believers and potential enemies of philosophical thought by concealing his real opinions beneath a disguise based upon orthodoxy. The only sort of reader who can hope to understand the text has to approach it very carefully, linking disparate passages together and examining the contradictions and evasions which pervade the text. In his introduction to the text Strauss suggests that the *Guide* is 'a book written by a Jew for Jews' ('How to begin', p.xiv), and he refuses to accept that it is a philosophical work. Here we will argue by contrast that the *Guide* is entirely philosophical in both content and form, and it presents within the context of a particular religion issues and problems which are universal in scope. The fact that its author is Jewish and its intended audience also Jewish is as relevant or irrelevant as the fact that the author of the *Summa Theologica* is Catholic and its intended audience is Catholic, or that the author of the *Incoherence of the Incoherence* is Muslim and its audience also Muslim. We have to take account of the cultural context within which all these texts have been produced, but this should not lead us to regard them as anything else but serious philosophy. They take their examples from a particular religion, and they use problems which arise within a particular theological tradition, but they are not thereby to be characterized as specifically religious texts. They involve argument and theory which is limited in interest by no religion or faith, since they extend our understanding of important aspects of our language and its possibilities.

Now, when one considers the historical conditions in which Maimonides lived and the difficulties which confronted him on every side, within as well as without his own community, it is tempting to fall into the trap of looking for hidden genuine views under the open apparent arguments and conclusions in his writings. He was brought up in a culture which exemplified concealment of one's real views from either the orthodox interpretation of faith or from a different but politically dominant religion. His own rather hectic history must have made him doubly aware of the importance of remaining discreet about his real religious commitments. When one looks at the *Guide* one finds that it is indeed full of remarks about allegory, metaphor, linguistic confusion and contradiction, parables and primary and secondary meanings, and one might conclude that

7

here is evidence of Maimonides' concern with protecting himself
from the consequences of a frank announcement of his views. On the
other hand, these topics could be taken to represent Maimonides'
philosophical concern with explaining how the nature of language
is transformed by its use in religious contexts, and how important
it is for us to distinguish clearly between our point of view and that
of the deity. Maimonides certainly was discreet, and the *Guide* would
no doubt have taken a different form had it been written in a
different society at a different time. Maimonides would himself have
been the first to admit this. Yet this does not detract from the clear
exposition of difficult philosophical topics in the text, topics on
which the author frequently shares his radical views with the reader.

There can be no doubt that Maimonides had a detailed grasp of
the works of his philosophical and theological predecessors. In a
letter to his translator Samuel ibn Tibbon he remarks:

> The works of Aristotle are the roots and foundations of all works
> on the sciences. But they cannot be understood except with the
> help of commentaries, those of Alexander of Aphrodisias, those
> of Themistius and those of Averroes.

> (*Int*, p.lix)

He contrasts Aristotle with Plato, where the latter is said to have
written in parables and not really contributed anything which is
not to be found in Aristotle. He expresses great admiration for
Farabi and ibn Bajja, and limited appreciation of ibn Sina
(Avicenna). What this suggests is that Maimonides is more attuned
to a form of Aristotelianism which is as far from neo-Platonic
accretions as could be achieved at a time when neo-Platonism
formed part of the language in which the process of philosophy
took place. We shall see later what significance his adherence to
Aristotelian philosophy entails, but it is worth pointing out at this
stage that Maimonides is indicating that he will seek to pursue the
form of philosophical analysis which contains the least possible
theological material. Neo-Platonism involves working with concepts
which are thoroughly imbued with concepts and principles that are
easily related to religious concepts, and Maimonides prefers to work
from philosophical principles which are as pure and logical as
possible, in order to achieve a more satisfactory logical demonstration to religious conclusions. This is why he indicates his admiration for Farabi and ibn Bajja, and the Greek commentators,

together with their distinguished follower, Averroes. This group of thinkers tried to follow Aristotelian premises and methods to arrive at a greater clarification of controversial issues relating to questions of religion, language and the human point of view, and some of the conclusions they reached were full of difficulties for believers. For example, in the *Commentary on the Nicomachean Ethics* Farabi is said to have labelled the belief in a life after death as 'old wives' tales' (*I*, pp. 91, 188). Ibn Bajja wrote frequently of the desirability of a withdrawal by the philosopher from the life of the state and the community when conditions are not propitious for the pursuit of that rational enterprise. The Greek commentators analysed Aristotle's views on the nature of the soul and came out with conclusions which differ from each other and have radical implications for a simplistic religious understanding of that notion. They all adhere to a model of the natural world which implies the need for a total change in the accepted understanding of miracles, prophecy and the relationship between our world and its creator. Maimonides' was basing his approach upon the school of philosophy which worked from the most awkward premises and methodology when considered from a religious point of view, and he was obviously perfectly aware that this was his stance and the only stance which he felt intellectually able to adopt.

It is noticeable that in his list of recommended authors and his comments on those to be avoided, he favours those who are thoroughly within the Peripatetic tradition and rejects anyone else, regardless of their religious and national affiliation. This leads him to refer critically to Jewish philosophers and thinkers by contrast with his attitude to Greek and Muslin authorities. Although the *Guide* is indeed written in such a way as only to attract initially Jewish readers, given the prevalence of passages from the Bible, Talmud, and commentaries on both together with examples of practices and rituals in Judaism, it is a text redolent with the issues and concerns of *falsafa* in its purest sense. The book is nominally written for a particular individual, either Joseph ben Judah or Joseph ibn Sham'ūn, a pupil of his, who was in some difficulty reconciling the letter of the law with the discoveries of natural science and Aristotelian philosophy. The way in which Maimonides addresses the text to this individual should not be seen as an esoteric device to restrict the meaning of the text to only a particular type of individual, but rather an indication of the sort of audience the text has in mind:

> I had a high opinion of you because of your strong desire for inquiry and because of what I had observed in your poems of your powerful longing for speculative matters ... When thereupon you read under my guidance texts dealing with the science of astronomy and prior to that texts dealing with mathematics, which is necessary as an introduction to astronomy, my joy in you increased because of the excellence of your mind and the quickness of your grasp. I saw that your longing for mathematics was great, and hence I let you train yourself in that science, knowing where you would end. When thereupon you read under my guidance texts dealing with the art of logic, my hopes fastened upon you, and I saw that you are one worthy to have the secrets of the prophetic books revealed to you so that you would consider in them that which perfect men ought to consider ... Then I saw that you demanded of me additional knowledge and asked me to make clear to you certain things pertaining to divine matters, to inform you of the intentions of the *mutakallimūn* [theologians] in this respect, and to let you know whether their methods were demonstrative ... As I also saw that you had already acquired some smattering of this subject from other people and were perplexed ... Yet I did not cease ... enjoining upon you to approach matters in an orderly manner. My purpose in this was that the truth should be established in your mind according to the proper methods.
>
> (*GP* Dedication, 3–4)

This dedication is very important, since it specifies quite clearly exactly what the purpose of the *Guide* is. The purpose is to explain in a logical and ordered way all that can be known about metaphysical problems. Maimonides is going to criticize the way in which the theologians address these problems, and his critique is based upon their lack of logical rigour in their arguments. As an Aristotelian, Maimonides will try to produce arguments which are demonstrative in form, which use necessary and true premises, and which apply them via a valid argument procedure to produce necessary and true conclusions. Theologians tend to employ less rigorous argument schemata, and especially dialectical arguments, whereby they start with premises which are probably true or generally accepted as true, and they will arrive at conclusions which are limited in their universality through the limitations of the premises. Since they use such poor material in their construction of arguments, it is hardly surprising that different sets of theologians can produce different conclusions starting from the same premises, and this results in the sort of perplexity to which Maimonides refers in his address to Joseph. Maimonides will attempt to dissolve that perplexity by pointing to the demonstrative arguments which should be employed in resolving metaphysical issues, and, as we shall see, a completely different and higher level of perplexity will arise.

This strategy is entirely in keeping with the style of *falsafa*. Many commentators imply that the *Guide* is a unique text and Maimonides is engaged upon a devious and extraordinary task. The reality is far from such extravagant conjecture. In his *Incoherence of the Incoherence* Averroes adopts what is in many ways the same approach as his fellow Andalusian Maimonides. In that book he criticizes the arguments which Ghazali and the Ash'arite theologians produce to demolish Aristotelian philosophy. He sets out to prove that those arguments are not demonstrative, but are rather dialectical or even worse, rhetorical, poetic or sophistical (*A*, p. 10). Averroes condemns the theologians for using a style of discourse which seems to prove their points but which on the contrary only haphazardly achieves the results they aim at, and as a consequence falls into the danger of diminishing the status of intellectual reasoning itself, or the religion which it seeks to set on firm rational foundations. What is required is a precise analysis of the different forms of discourse which theologians and philosophers use in their statements, and a differentiation of those forms from the language of lawyers, politicians and so on. We can then examine what criteria are appropriate to these different discourses and establish on a sure rational basis at least some aspects of faith. Hence the emphasis upon different forms of language, different proof methods in varying contexts, and the importance of bringing order and analysis into the study of religion and its social implications.

Towards the end of the *Guide* Maimonides has a particularly fine example of how he distinguishes between different kinds of audience. He produces a parable in which he describes a variety of routes which people adopt in their search for knowledge, which he identifies as ultimately a search for God. Like the address to Joseph at the beginning of the book, it is worth quoting this parable at some length:

> The ruler is in his palace, and all his subjects are partly within the city and partly outside the city. Of those who are within the city, some have turned their backs upon the ruler's habitation, their faces being turned another way. Others seek to reach the ruler's habitation, turn towards it, and desire to enter it and to stand before him, but up to now they have not yet seen the wall of the habitation. Some of those who seek to reach it have come up to the habitation and walk around it searching for the gate. Some of them have entered the gate and walk about in the antechambers. Some of them have entered the inner court of the habitation and have come to be with the king, in one and the same place with him, namely, in the ruler's habitation. But their having come into the inner part of the habitation does not mean that they see the ruler or speak to him. For after their coming into the inner part of the habitation, it is indispensable that they should make another effort; then they will be in the presence of the ruler, see him from afar or from nearby, or hear the ruler's speech or speak to him.
>
> (*GP* III, 51; 618)

In his explanation of the parable the people who are outside the city are those without a faith based upon either religion or reason. These people are the most distant from any hope of knowledge or understanding of the most important issues which concern them and their world. Those who are inside the city but have their backs turned on the ruler's dwelling are people who use reason or tradition to attain their grasp of reality, but have made some grievous error in their reasoning, or based their beliefs upon an erroneous tradition. Maimonides suggests that the more they think, the further away they stray from the ruler's dwelling. This is because their ideas are based upon a fallacy, either self-induced or as a part of a religious or theological tradition, and the more they work out conclusions based upon that fallacy, the more awry they go. Then he comments that 'Those who seek to reach the ruler's habitation and to enter it, but never see the ruler's habitation, are the multitude of the adherents of the Law, I refer to the ignoramuses who observe the commandments' (*GP* III, 51; 119). This seems an extraordinary way to describe the vast majority of the community of believers; all

12

those people who faithfully adhere to the requirements and rituals of their religion but who do not for one reason or another speculate concerning the reasons for these laws are labelled as ignoramuses. Clearly these are people who would find much more of interest in Maimonides' legal works than in his philosophical analyses.

People who manage to reach the ruler's dwelling and walk around it are the lawyers who base their opinions upon a well-based tradition, but do not question the foundation of that tradition. Then we reach the group of people who can enter the antechambers, those who engage in speculative thought about the most fundamental issues in religion. Maimonides claims that:

> He, however, who has achieved demonstration, to the extent that that is possible, of everything that may be demonstrated; and who has ascertained in divine matters, to the extent that that is possible, everything that may be ascertained; and who has come close to certainty in those matters in which one can only come close to it – has come to be with the ruler in the inner part of the habitation.
>
> (*GP* III, 51; 619)

He continues this point by arguing that if one restricts one's investigations to mathematics and logic one will remain outside the house, while if one moves onto the study of natural science one can get inside. If this study is perfected along with metaphysical knowledge, as far as this is possible for human beings, one is successful in attaining the inner chamber where the ruler lives. The analogy is that our understanding of the deity and his characteristics, in so far as we can achieve such understanding (which as we shall see is very limited for Maimonides), can only come about through a structured and demonstrative intellectual route. It is not to be achieved by flashes of divine inspiration, nor chance investigation, nor even by following faithfully the religious and legal requirements of one's faith. Only a careful and well-organized rational plan will enable us to achieve the sort of personal intellectual development which will take us in the right direction. It is the purpose of the *Guide* to help those readers who are appropriately constituted in their intellectual abilities and interests establish their place on this route.

Maimonides wrote his book and virtually all his other philosophical works in Arabic but in Hebrew characters. In fact, many of his rabbinic books are also in Arabic, which is an excellent indication of the prevalence of Arabic among the Jewish communities in the Islamic world. As far as his more popular works are concerned, such as the *Letter to Yemen*, for example, in which he seeks to succour the beleaguered Jewish community in that region, it is clearly important to write in such a way that the majority of the community would understand when, as intended, the *Letter* was read out at public meetings of that community. The fact that on his death in 1204 there were large-scale demonstrations of grief among some communities of Jews suggests that there was no problem in most people understanding his more popular writings. It would have been difficult for Maimonides to write his philosophical works in Hebrew given the paucity of philosophical tradition in that language, whereas Arabic provided a friendly medium for both scholarly and ordinary debate. It was the sort of science, theology and philosophy then current in the Islamic world which led to the sort of perplexity which Maimonides wished to resolve, and Arabic is the appropriate language for such an enterprise.

It is often pointed out by commentators that the *Guide* is a most unusual book. Indeed, this point is often developed to add weight to the theory that it is an esoteric work which can only be approached cautiously and with one's eyes forever combing the text for contradiction, dissimulation, and deviousness. This is an interpretation which has misled much of the work on Maimonides in the last few decades. It has already been suggested that there are marked similarities between the form of the *Guide* and of a philosophical text within the tradition of *falsafa*. The text I chose was Averroes' *Incoherence of the Incoherence*, and that is a rather useful example, since it is not concerned with purely philosophical topics. Its subject matter is the attack upon Peripatetic philosophy by the Ash'arite theologian Ghazali. In fact, the nature of this subject matter has led some commentators to argue that Averroes' book is not supposed to be demonstrative, but is rather dialectical in structure and not a frank explication of the author's real views. This is as preposterous a notion as that of the nonphilosophical and esoteric nature of the *Guide*. Both books seek to challenge the very serious challenge which Ghazali hurled against the *falāsifa*, namely, the apparent impossibility of reconciling a meaningful notion of God with their account of the world and its operation (*I*, pp. 38–41: *A*, p. 14). This particular difficulty runs right through the *Guide* as well, and is treated by

Maimonides in a different way from Averroes' approach, based as that treatment is upon a different theory of language. In his attack upon philosophy Ghazali argued that the philosophers commit two types of error. Their arguments are not acceptable even on their own account of demonstrative argument, and they cannot incorporate in their description of the world and its maker the traditional features of the sort of deity present in Islam, and it might be added, in Judaism and Christianity. Ghazali suggests very cleverly that the way in which the philosophers use the notion of God pays lip-service to the power and significance of the individual referred to by the name but in practice leaves no room for a powerful and significant deity to affect and know his creation. When we come to consider Maimonides' arguments on this issue we shall see in more detail how Ghazali tried to establish his points, but it is worth saying here that there can be no real doubt that Maimonides understood the importance and force of Ghazali's approach. One of the notable aspects of Ghazali is his readiness to use the tools of philosophy – demonstrative argument – to argue against philosophy, and this must have impressed an admirer of philosophical technique such as Maimonides. Ghazali's adherence to philosophical methodology led me to describe him as a *failasūf* malgré lui (*I*, pp. 15–16) and his intellectual spirit stalks the *Guide*. This again is another indication of the distinctness of the work, incorporating as it does both the arguments of the chief opponent of the *falāsifa* while following the general approach of a philosophical text at the same time.

An aspect of Maimonides which we must not overlook, despite its general lack of comment among the commentators, is his Spanishness, in the sense of his cultural dependence upon Islamic Spain. His Arabic name is Abū 'Imrān Mūsā ibn 'Ubaydallāh al-Qortobī (i.e. his father is referred to as from Cordoba) and when he signed letters and documents it generally takes the form of 'Moses son of rabbi Maimun the Spaniard'. This is not just a matter of stylistic convenience. The philosophical authorities which he is prepared to accept are more from the west of the Islamic empire (ibn Bajja, ibn Rushd) than from the east (ibn Sina) (*Int*, p. iv). It is worth mentioning too that many of his most ardent opponents in the Jewish intellectual community were to be found in the centres of Talmudic study in Iraq. The intellectual climate in Spanish circles involved a fresh approach to the way in which the traditional centres of Islam had dealt with metaphysical and scientific issues. For the first thirty years of his life Maimonides lived in Spain and the *Maghrib* (North Africa) where the cultural influences were thoroughly Andalusian. This spirit is even more confidently expressed by Averroes, but it is certainly there in Maimonides. How is this spirit to be characterized? Briefly, it might be said that it specifies a return to basic issues and a refusal to fall under the spell of the accretions to such issues which had taken place in those parts of the world with an older and more conservative cultural tradition. In philosophy the Spanish thinkers are noted for their concern at getting back to the problems which Aristotle considered and omitting as much neo-Platonic and theological cladding which had been placed upon Aristotelianism as they could. In the *Guide* Maimonides can be observed to return time and time again to the same issues, and the detail in the book is merely an elaboration of these issues.

What are these issues? They come down to the question of how we can use our ordinary language to make sense of statements which appear to elude the descriptive potential of such language. What is the link between the assertion that we think and see, and the claim that God thinks and sees? What is the relationship between a divine and an ordinary law? When a ruler is powerful and wise he establishes a system of law which punishes and rewards citizens fairly entirely on the basis of their deserts. We know from our experience that sometimes the innocent apparently suffer illness and financial disaster while the evil prosper; how can we reconcile the claim that this goes on and yet there is an omnipotent deity who wisely and kindly looks after the interests of his creatures? What is the relationship between the claim that a ruler is powerful and wise, and the claim that God is powerful and wise? This after all is what perplexes the intelligent reader, the person who has some mastery of science and who finds it difficult to reconcile what he knows about the structure of the world and its appropriate analysis with the claims of religion. He understands that Aristotle and his followers give a particular meaning to the phenomenon of prophecy, for example, which identifies it largely with natural phenomena, and he accepts the account of prophecy which is cashed in terms of the specific qualities of the individual prophet, rather than in terms of God granting that individual specific powers through his divine will. He wonders how he can reconcile the claim that prophecy is a natural event with the claim that it is only available through divine grace. This basic problem of reconciling two different ways of describing the same thing is very much the theme of the *Guide*, and arises on every page of the text in one form or another.

Many commentators of the *Guide* seek to dramatize the problem by representing it as a complete incompatibility between being a believer, in this case a Jew, and being a philosopher (see in particular Strauss 'How to begin', p. xiv). They argue that the Jewish religion proscribes the sort of theoretical inquiry explicitly carried out in philosophy, and that Maimonides was quite aware that the very writing of the *Guide* contravened all manner of religious prohibitions. Such a view is, of course, ridiculous. Mainline Judaism, like Islam and Christianity, is wary of believers raising questions which cannot be resolved within the confines of the faith, but they all assume that there is no essential contradiction between religion and reason. It may well be that an imprudent enquirer will raise issues which he cannot understand within the context of his faith, and he is recommended to rest content with the ordinary religious understanding of such questions. Hence the suggestion which runs right throughout *falsafa* that the ordinary believer should not meddle in issues which he cannot fully understand, since it leads to a weakening of faith in religion or a feeling of suspicion towards philosophy. There is no reason to believe that Maimonides was consciously doing what he ought not to be doing, and therefore had to conceal his message from the ordinary reader. The apparent conflict between reason and religion is apparent to most believers who would be astounded to find that their religion forbade any discussion of possible difficulties in reconciling one with the other. The perplexity which the reader feels is related to such a conflict, and Maimonides addresses himself to such a reader. He uses arguments and explains texts in his analysis; he does not proceed by assembling contradictions and repetitions which mislead the naïve reader and instruct the more intelligent concerning his real purpose. The account presented in this book is based upon the principle that Maimonides intends to present clear and decisive arguments in favour of his theses. The suggestion that there is a hidden doctrine is entirely discounted in the chapters which follow, and if the book succeeds it will show that we must address ourselves fully to Maimonides' arguments and not to any putative hidden doctrines which owe far more to the imagination of most of his commentators than to anything we can find in the text.

2

How can we talk about God?

One of the most controversial aspects of Maimonides' philosophical thought is his account of the divine attributes. One might imagine that this is an aspect of a remote and obscure controversy of little interest beyond the Middle Ages. This assumption would be an error, though, since Maimonides' thinking on this issue is just as relevant today as in the past, and its significance is not limited to the question of the divine attributes, but extends to his theory of meaning itself. It is hardly surprising that this theory should have received so much attention, since it has very radical implications. If he is right, no positive attributes can be predicated of God. The only sorts of positive characteristics which we can apply to the deity are taken to be actions and the effects of those actions, but only in a very limited sense. Not in the sense that one can look at these words on this page and infer that there was an author who originally wrote them and was interested in a particular set of problems. My actions allow other people to form reasonable judgments about the sort of person I am; God's actions allow nothing of the sort, on this theory. All that we are permitted to know is that God does *not* have the sorts of qualities which we might wish to believe.

It is important to set this issue within its context. There had for a long time been conflict in the Islamic world over the nature of the divine attributes, with the Mu'tazila emphasizing the absolute unity and indivisibility of God by holding the divine predicates to be nothing more than different names of God. Their opponents took the references in the Koran to predicates such as 'life', 'knowledge' and 'power' as real eternal things in God which are both distinct from his essence and from his name (*I*, pp. 11–12). This theological conflict went hand-in-hand with a philosophical debate, namely, how are we to talk in a meaningful sense about a subject so different from our normal experience as is the case with God? A transcendent being possesses characteristics which must be very different from the contents of our everyday world, and we might well wonder how we are to think of such a being. Of course, there are indications in religious texts which act as a guide in this respect, but these only go so far. One seems to be placed in something of a dilemma in using language to describe God. Either God appears to be something of a Greek god or a Superman, just like us but more so, or he is so distinct from us that we cannot speak about him at all. Neither alternative is very attractive, and not just from a religious point of view. The notion of God which exists in religious language would not be adequately characterized on either the Superman or the absolutely transcendent description. The former does not make enough of the distinction between God and man, while the latter makes too much of that distinction. On the other hand, there is obviously something in the concept of God which borrows from both alternatives. The idea that God is indeed in possession of perfectly comprehensible qualities such as power and will is important in the sense that he is regarded as omnipotent and able to decide on what he is to do. There are many scriptural passages which give evidence of his ability to know, will and do things. Any attempt at challenging this sort of language might be regarded as an attempt at denying the reality of a God who intervenes in significant ways in human affairs.

An excellent example of this concern is to be found in many of the criticisms which Ghazali makes of the work of the *falāsifa* (*I*, pp. 38–58: *A*, pp. 15–81). We can learn a lot from the title he gives to his 'Third Discussion' in his *Tahafut al-falāsifa* (Incoherence of the philosophers). It is 'the demonstration of their confusion in saying that God is the agent and the maker of the world and that the world is his product and act, and the demonstration that these expressions are in their system only metaphors without any real sense' (*TT*, p. 147). Ghazali's point here is that we can only call God a real agent if he can be taken to form decisions, carry them out and have the will and purpose to bring about certain changes in the world. We must think of God acting rather like us, except that he has far greater knowledge and power. It is very important for Ghazali that a meaningful deity can only be a real agent if he

19

acts 'through will and through choice' (*TT*, p. 156). Ghazali continues by suggesting that

> our aim in this question is to show that you philosophers use those venerable names without justification, and that God, according to you, is not a true agent, nor the world truly his act, and that you are applying this word metaphorically – not in its real sense. This has now been shown.
>
> (*TT*, p. 171).

In his response Averroes has to try to show that 'the philosophers . . . only affirm that He does not will in the way that man wills' (*TT*, p. 160), and this brings out an important feature of the debate, namely, that it is not essentially a debate about the nature of God, but rather about meaning. Ghazali has a view of meaning which places the stress upon univocity. That is, he expects the terms we apply to God to be the same terms which we apply to non-divine creatures, and the activities we credit the deity with differ only in scope from many of our own activities. Indeed, he goes further in arguing that any attempt at interpreting the properties of God as equivocal or ambiguous or metaphorical is a subtle means of attacking the notion of God itself. This discussion tends to centre on the issue of the nature of the divine attributes, but it has a far wider focus. It encompasses the entire question of the relationship between religious and ordinary language, a relationship which Averroes and Maimonides seek to explicate time and again in their work. It is important that we try to become a bit clearer on the precise nature of this controversial issue.

In Averroes' *Middle Commentary* on Aristotle's *Categories* he suggests:

> Aristotle states: Things whose names are common, that is, equivocal, are things that have nothing general or common to them except for the name, while the definition of each, which states its essence in consideration of the meaning of the equivocal name, differs from the definition of the other and is peculiar to its own definiendum. An example is the name 'animal' when predicated both of a drawing of a man and of a rational man, for the definitions of these two differ, and the two having nothing general and in common except for the name, that is, our calling them both animal.
>
> (*Middle Commentary*, p. 32)

The importance of the doctrine of equivocation lies in its application to the issue of divine attributes, and ultimately to the relationship between religious and ordinary language. Aristotle makes a distinction between two types of equivocal terms, pure equivocals and *pros hen* equivocals. The former share only the name, while the latter describes some similarity in the objects compared which forms the reason for claiming that they both share the same name. Actually, Aristotle is quite careful in not claiming that the only thing which the man and the drawing of the man have in common is the name, since he adds to his discussion the phrase 'but the definition of being corresponding to the name is different' (*Categories* 1 a 4). Averroes appears undecided about whether to agree with Aristotle here or whether to argue that the relationship between the picture of the man and the man himself is completely equivocal. On the whole he tends to the view that the language we use to describe the attributes of God takes the form of *pros hen* equivocals, since if they were to be entirely equivocal, there would be nothing in common between our religious and our ordinary language except the words themselves, while if they were to be univocal they would inevitably lead to an analysis in terms of a genus and species, which in turn would imply multiplicity within the unity of the deity.

Averroes argues that God is the exemplar of all things, and contains them in a complete way, since 'his essence, according to the philosophers, contains all intellects and existents in a nobler and more perfect way than they all possess in reality' (*TT*, p. 202). There are clearly problems with calling God a thing in the way in which we call ordinary objects things, and Averroes argues that God is paradigmatically a thing, while everything else enjoys only a derivative degree of substance. The concept of God has a special status which defies description as though it were an ordinary concept definable in terms of type and qualities. Were God to be thus definable, he would consist of a number of attributes which made up a plurality, in the same way that we consist of thinking, wanting, acting, and so on. This would be an error, though. We tend to separate things which exist as a unity into their parts, as though those parts could enjoy separate existence. When we think about immaterial things we use the same sort of language as when thinking about an everyday object, but these similarities in language should not obscure the fact that we are using the same terms in different ways, indeed, in analogical ways. It is acceptable, although rather

21

peculiar, to call a fire warm, since a fire can be taken to be a paradigm of warmth, a perfect instance of this quality which is found in other phenomena to a lesser degree. A hot water bottle is warm because of its resemblance to the warmth of a fire, and the principles which are directly present in the warmth of the fire are to a degree present in the warmth of the bottle. The fire is warm in the fullest possible sense, and the hot water bottle is warm in a derivative sense.

This theory of meaning is designed to help Averroes sidestep the position of Ghazali which emphasizes the notion of a deity existing without attributes. According to Averroes, when we apply predicates to the deity we apply them to only one genus of thing, because that very special genus exemplifies in the best possible way all those predicates. There is only one God who brings about the world and everything in it, and all the predicates which we apply to ourselves are mere shadows of those which originate in the deity. God's properties are essentially part of his being in a way that is unique; our predicates are accidentally characteristics of us. They come and go, we change and become different sorts of people, but God is unchanging and his properties do not change either. This solves the problem of reconciling the essential simplicity of the notion of God with the fact that he has properties, since those properties can be regarded as essential aspects of him, which in turn make possible the application of properties to aspects of the world in general. We tend to think of God as someone rather like us, but more so, and so we imagine that he has properties in much the same way as we do, but this is the effect of our imagination separating out features which are really logically inseparable. When we talk about God we must have in mind a being whose properties are an essential and indivisible feature of his essence.

It is a leading principle of Averroes' philosophy that when ordinary people and sophisticated philosophers know certain propositions about religion to be true, they all know the same thing. They all know that God understands everything there is to understand about the world, and this is made clearer to the masses by the ascription of seeing and hearing to God. The philosophers realize that this cannot be meant literally, since God has no body. Precisely how he knows and understands is not known to either group, and is unimportant. This comes out nicely in Averroes' treatment of the protracted controversy between the Mu'tazilites and the Ash'arites on whether the divine attributes are identical with God's essence, or distinct from it. The Ash'arite view is that the attributes are distinct from God's essence and this implies that God consists of essence and predicate, in other words, a multiplicity. The Mu'tazilites argue for the identity of deity and attributes (*TT*, p. 354; also p. 446 and p. 149). It is something of a theme of Averroes that we are led by Islam to acknowledge the very profound difference which must exist between ourselves and the deity. The difference is to be explained, as we have seen, in terms of God possessing certain attributes in their most perfect and complete forms, which we can only be said to share in an equivocal manner. Averroes argues that one of the chief virtues of Islam as a faith is its capacity to employ highly imaginative and effective imagery to get its point across. It makes plain to the widest possible group of people what it is they ought to do and believe. The necessity to behave in morally appropriate ways is clearly high on Averroes' agenda of the criteria of a successful religion, and Islam, with its blend of inspiration and reason (*TT*, p. 584) fulfils this requirement well.

Averroes sets his face firmly against the sort of literalism produced by Ghazali. The latter is only satisfied with a deity who can be described in the sorts of ways in which we can describe things of our everyday experience. This is not to say, of course, that in his opinion God is to be identified with ordinary objects. Ghazali wants God to be identified with aspects of our lives which matter to us, rather than having the sort of nebulous and almost superfluous status suggested by the *falāsifa*. Maimonides goes one step further than Averroes in the response to Ghazali. For Averroes there is an equivocal link between our ordinary language and our religious language. For Maimonides there is no connection at all between the two. In Chapters 51 to 60 of the first Book of the *Guide of the Perplexed* he argues that no positive predicates at all can be applied to God. We can talk about God's actions and the effects of those actions, but we cannot move from language about the existence of things to any definite language about the nature of God's existence. Maimonides asks:

> How then can a relation be represented between Him and what is other than He when there is no notion comprising in any respect both of the two, inasmuch as existence is . . . affirmed of

Him . . . and of what is other than He merely by way of absolute equivocation. How could there subsist a relation between Him . . . and any of the things created by Him, given the immense difference between them with regard to the true reality of their existence, than which there is no greater difference?

(*GP* I, 52; 117–8)

For Maimonides, the use of the same name to describe divine and contingent phenomena is misleading if we are led to believe that there is any resemblance between that term's role in divine and ordinary language. So when we look at the development of the theory of meaning from Ghazali to Maimonides we observe a move from univocity to complete equivocation, with Averroes coming somewhere in the middle with his more moderate account of relative equivocation.

Averroes' account of meaning underpins his well-known theory of the existence of a variety of paths to the truth. The relatively loose connection between the use of similar names permits him to discuss the difficulties involved in grasping what those names mean. Their meanings differ depending upon the context within which they are used, although they are not completely different and distinct. There is a thread of meaning connecting the different uses which extends from the divine exemplar to the temporal imitation. If we regard these terms as clear and univocal then we will get into the sorts of difficulties experienced by Avicenna in explaining how a simple deity could embody a multiplicity of attributes, and of how the essence of a thing is independent of its existence. If we regard these terms as completely equivocal, as Maimonides does, then we shall have the difficulty of knowing what to say about an entirely ineffable deity. One of the advantages of Averroes' approach is the interesting support it provides for his account of a point of view. In his work there is a continual contrast between different points of view, not only between God's point of view and the human point of view, but also a differentiation between the standpoints of a whole variety of different human beings based upon their forms of reasoning. In his *Faṣl al-maqāl* (Decisive treatise) there is the interesting distinction between different sorts of people with different levels of intellectual ability, yet all of whom use similar language to talk about issues of mutual significance, such as their religion, the deity, the after-life and so on. This language clearly differs when it is used by a philosopher and when it is used by an ordinary member of the religious community, yet it is not entirely different. There exist links in meaning between different uses of the same name so that it makes sense to talk about these usages as coming under a certain general description. It is rather like pointing to the different views which a doctor and a patient have of a particular disease (a common example in the Islamic world, where medicine and philosophy frequently go hand-in-hand). The views and understandings in this case are different, yet they relate to the same phenomenon, and have enough in common to be regarded as different views of the same object. Similarly, an ordinary believer has a different grasp of his faith and its foundations than does a philosopher, and our language is capable of containing a whole variety of such views, ranging from the most accurate and demonstrative to the most poetic and figurative. He takes this to show that equivocation in language is not something to be rejected as such. This aspect of our language must be accepted since it is a feature of our lives in a world with different people living in a community with a whole range of ends and interests in prospect.

As we have seen, Ghazali condemns the suggestion that equivocation is a feature of the relationship between our language describing God and our language describing the ordinary world. He regards this as an attack upon the notion of God as a powerful and all-encompassing individual. Maimonides, by contrast, sees any suggestion that this relationship is not entirely equivocal as reducing God to the status of a powerful human being. In his reply, Averroes would argue that equivocation is an inevitable aspect of our language since that language has to describe a wide range of views using the same name. We must respect the different uses of the same word because they represent different points of view – different points of view of the same object. It is an error to represent some uses as essentially more accurate than others. Averroes tries to show how it is possible for one thing to be described in a variety of ways, which neither Ghazali nor Maimonides can do on his account.

Why was Maimonides drawn to arguing for such an extreme view of the lack of relationship between religious and nonreligious language? He felt that once it had been established that God was entirely incorporeal, simple, and immutable there can be no sense in linking our everyday language about matter, complexity, and will to the deity. In the first place, God has no essence in the sense that we can define him (*GP* I, 51–2). When we come to know what particular things are we relate the name to a combination of qualities, but this cannot be done to the notion of God, since he is not divisible into a collection of qualities (*GP* I, 52) and has no properties that are connected in a contingent way to him. He cannot be affected or influenced by anything else in existence (*GP* I, 55) and there is no possibility of even describing him by relating him to anything else (*GP* I, 52, 56). We cannot even understand what it means to talk about God existing, if by this we mean that he shares this state with us (*GP* I, 56). This is a very radical doctrine. It quite clearly implies that there are problems in knowing whom we believe in if we believe in God. When we pray we do not produce any effect on God, we can establish no sort of connection with him. God cannot even notice the fact that people pray to him given his complete independence from any connection with the world of corruption and generation. The idea of God possessing an attitude of care and concern for 'his' creatures so prevalent in the liturgy of both Islam and Judaism is accordingly inappropriate and empty.

Before we explore some of the implications of this doctrine, it is worth spending a little more time on exactly how Maimonides thinks he has established it on a firm footing. The first way of applying predicates to a subject is through finding and defining the general species to which the subject belongs. This method is clearly inapplicable to the deity once we accept that it is inappropriate to think of him as a member of a species. The second way is to think of the subject having a number of characteristics, which falls foul of the notion of God as a complete unity. The third way takes these characteristics to be nonessential parts of the subject, which is even less appropriate than characterizing him through a combination of essential predicates. Even talking about the bare existence of God is problematic given the difference between his form of existence and that to which we are accustomed. God is the only thing in existence which exists necessarily. Everything else exists because of its relation to something else, ultimately, to God himself. This different form of existence is not something which we can clearly grasp merely by contrasting it with our everyday notion of existence. We are used to things existing in a complex network of relationships with other things, and the idea of something existing and at the same time completely escaping this framework is difficult to grasp.

So difficult, Maimonides claims, that it almost rules out the use of the term 'existence' when talking about God (*GP* I, 52).

Can we refer to God at all, then, on Maimonides' account? The position appears to be doubtful, but he does allow just one type of predication of God. We can talk about God's actions, and this is because he appears to think that there is a different logical structure to sentences with action phrases in them and sentences with predicates in general (*Treatise on Logic*, ch. 3). The relevance of the distinction is that actions can be distinguished from ordinary predicates or characteristics, because they do not necessarily imply a plurality in the agent. We have to bear in mind here the great differences between the agency of God and human agency. For us actions are evidence of complexity and mutability. We make decisions, change our minds, are affected by exterior and interior events, wait for something to happen before we do something, and so on. For God, by contrast, actions are a reflection of his absolute simplicity and essence. They are not arrived at arbitrarily and haphazardly, but are rather unique events which represent the optimum organization of the natural world. Although we can talk about God bringing things about this does not mean we can relax the restriction on referring to his changing or wanting something to take place. We can talk about God acting, but must be aware at all times that our language here is entirely equivocal and bears no relation apart from the use of the same words to the meaning of those words in the different human and divine contexts (*GP* I, 54–6). It would be better to abandon all positive language about what God does, because we are always likely to fall into the trap of anthropomorphism. Even though we might accept that we are using the same terms in very different ways, there is a tendency for many people to relax their intellectual grasp on this distinction and sink into inappropriate ways of thinking about God. Most people feel the need to weaken the absolute distinction which Maimonides tries to establish because, in his terms, they are not intellectually developed enough to do away with the crutch of a simplistic view of religion.

We must recall here that Maimonides' extreme view is an aspect of the radical nature of his theory of meaning. For Averroes and his philosophical predecessors Avicenna and Farabi, going back probably to Aristotle, a very different technique was used to allow for the distinction between religious and ordinary language. This technique prevented one from having to accept the use of language to describe religious events in the sort of way that Ghazali insisted it be used, in a more or less literal way. Ghazali threw down the challenge to the Peripatetic tradition that it pretends to believe in God and in divine influence on the world but refuses to allow any language to be used to describe these phenomena which make any real difference to the way in which the world is organized. The philosophers, he contends, insist on such a convoluted and limited context for divine influence as to negate its significance and identify it with natural events. They do not go about their task openly, but rather argue that religious language is metaphorical and equivocal, and has to be carefully differentiated from our everyday language. This has the effect of implying that divine influence over our lives and the world itself is not real but merely metaphorical, so that God does not in any clear and easily comprehensible way control his creation. Why bother to talk about God at all if we are not going to give him anything meaningful to do? Religious texts are far from hesitant in their ascription of characteristics to the deity, and when the philosophers start to raise objections to such ascriptions it looks very much like a roundabout way of criticizing the coherence of the religion itself (A, pp. 42–81).

Most of the philosophers had a ready answer to this form of attack on Peripateticism. They argued that the logical relationship between divine and ordinary language is along the lines of the *pros hen* notion of equivocation. On this view God possesses in the most perfect way the attributes which we only partially possess. For example, we are limited in our claims to knowledge to being affected by the external world, whereas God creates the contents of his knowledge at the same time as he is aware of it. We must rely on a piecemeal and fallible information-gathering process, yet by contrast, since God exemplifies the most perfect and indubitable form of wisdom, he knows in a perfect and complete sense. We know in a derivative sense, and our knowledge (such as it is) is made possible in the first place through divine activity itself.

This sort of approach may be found partially in Aristotle and extends through Farabi, Avicenna and Averroes, reaching Aquinas and the Christian scholastic tradition. Their response to the attack of the literalists is two-pronged. In the first place they argue, quite convincingly it would seem, that the attempt at interpreting the anthropomorphic language surrounding the deity as holding onto its ordinary sense is to go awry. Secondly, they are still able to attribute God with his normal set of qualities, but these must be interpreted as his qualities in a special way. This special way is not metaphorical in the sense that it is vague and indeterminate, which might be seen as threatening to a clear view of the divine characteristics. It is special because it represents the most perfect example of those qualities, and their more normal sense which we use when we apply them to ourselves is in fact derivative from their divine sense. This might be seen as a rather neat metaphor for the relationship between God and his creation.

Maimonides is entirely opposed to this way of resolving the issue. He accepts that there are some accidental features which a variety of subjects can share, so that a living person, a dead person and a statue may all have the same shape (*Treatise on Logic*, ch. 13). This form of analogy is useless when we try to get from ordinary language to religious language, though, since the simplicity of God means that he has no qualities at all in the sense that we understand having qualities. The whole point of using analogy to further the move from ordinary to religious language is that there is a degree of resemblance between the subjects referred to in both contexts, and Maimonides firmly sets his face against this possibility. The notion of God is an entirely different notion logically from the sorts of things we are accustomed to describing.

Before we consider the question of the validity of this approach we must examine some qualifications which Maimonides makes to it. As we have seen, he rather grudgingly accepts that it is slightly more appropriate to talk of God's actions as compared with his qualities. Again, and this time more confusingly, the *Guide* frequently refers to God in ways which its author seeks at other places to dismiss. For example, Moses is said to have grasped the essence of God (*GP* I, 3) and to have successfully prayed to God for his people's forgiveness (*GP* I, 54). God is said to have sent Moses out to make out of the Jewish people a kingdom of priests and a holy nation (*GP* III, 32). God punishes people (*GP* I, 10) and becomes angry with them (*GP* I, 29, 36). In many other places Maimonides reproduces with apparent agreement biblical passages in which the idea that God has a direct relationship with his creation is firmly expressed.

Again, when Maimonides discusses his view of the deity he provides a lot of detail which one might think difficult to reconcile with his view of God's essential transcendence. On his account of creation, God brought everything else into existence out of a state of non-existence in accordance with nothing other than his will. This appears to be his account of creation in the second book of the *Guide*. Similarly, in the third book he presents an account of God's knowledge which represents him as entirely omniscient, with a form of knowledge which is completely unified even though it encompasses phenomena belonging to a variety of species. His knowledge can range infinitely and does not change even when it encompasses changing things. One might well wonder how we could make these sorts of claims about someone who is absolutely unknowable to the human mind. As Reines puts the question, 'how can Maimonides know that God knows all things other than Himself by knowing His own essence, which would require Maimonides to have knowledge of that essence?' ('Maimonides' True Belief', p. 30). He pointedly asks with reference to Maimonides' account of creation:

> Since the nature of God's existence is entirely unknown to the human mind, how can Maimonides know the state in which God existed before the creation of the universe? Moreover, since God's essence is entirely unknown to humans, and His will and wisdom are one with his essence, how can Maimonides know it was through them God created the universe, or what it means to speak of God's will and wisdom? Similarly, since God's essence is unknown, how can Maimonides know God acted purposefully in creating the universe, and not through the necessity of His own essential nature? Furthermore, how does Maimonides know, since God's essence is unknown, that deity has not from all eternity been in the act of creation? Least of all, it would appear, that Maimonides can know the order in which deity created the universe and that He directly and personally determined the structure, direction, and velocity of each of the spheres.
>
> ('Maimonides' True Belief', p. 29)

Reines appears to make a very strong point here, and he manages to resolve it by arguing that the apparent incompatability between these different ways of talking is really an example of Maimonides' use of contradiction to put off the unsophisticated. This gets us into very murky territory indeed, but since commentators on Maimonides are so fond of this sort of move, it is necessary to consider it. Reines in particular suggests that Maimonides is here employing what the latter calls the seventh reason for contradiction, which is where contradictory premises are employed to set the minds of the unsophisticated at rest and at the same time stimulate the intellectual appetite of those philosophically trained. The assertions of the existence of a powerful and knowable deity to whom humans beings can appeal is clearly the sort of notion required by Rabbinic Judaism, and it cannot then be the object of the concealment enterprise. This must be the more rarified view of God, as someone about whom it is virtually impossible to make any meaningful positive comment at all. This latter is possibly destructive of what most people would count as religious faith, and should not be publicized to all and sundry. The wise will be able to see beneath the contradiction to the notion of the deity which Maimonides is setting up for their acceptance beneath the comforting veil of tradition.

However, we are not obliged to go in this direction. Reines argues that Maimonides' real view is that none of the arguments for God having particular characteristics is valid or compelling. Maimonides does indeed refer to his argument for divine creation *ex nihilo* as no more certain than Aristotle's contrary theory (*GP* II, 25). It is a mistake to conclude from this that in his arguments he is merely presenting views which are designed to accord with orthodoxy while concealing his very different real views. When he is hesitant in claiming that his arguments for God's creation *ex nihilo* and omniscience are demonstratively valid, he is not throwing them out as arguments, but rather limiting their impact to those who accept the premises. The premises of such arguments are the leading principles of religion, and will not be accepted by those who do not adhere to those principles in the first place. These principles differ from religion to religion, and are far from being the sort of premises used in demonstrative argument, which works with necessary statements to reach necessary conclusions. The type of argument which predominates in religion is dialectical, and perfectly valid as far as it goes (*I*, p. 143). The limitation with it is that it cannot go so far as to convince someone who is not prepared to accept the way in which the argument starts, i.e. the particular religious premises or propositions. Maimonides argues at some length for his view of divine creation and knowledge, and it is extraordinary to imply that this is nothing more than a cloak for his true beliefs about God. He is seeking to establish on philosophically secure grounds the sorts of claims which religious people make, and show how those claims can make sense even when analysed philosophically. How he does this will be elucidated in some detail in later sections.

It is obvious that the accounts which Maimonides gives of creation and divine knowledge are theoretically more complex than the scriptural claims about the effect of prayer, God's awareness of the contingent world, and his changing emotions which we mentioned earlier. Maimonides does indeed seem to endorse these descriptions too, and has little choice in the matter given their scriptural basis. How can he reconcile these sorts of statements with his argument for the indescribability of God in positive terms? He would claim that this sort of language is suitable for people who either had little ability to understand theoretical argument, or who had no time to enter into speculation concerning the proper interpretation of these passages. If they understand the import of such passages, what they are designed to produce in terms of action, then that is enough. In fact, like Averroes Maimonides stresses the potentially dangerous process of discussing theoretical problems about the interpretations of such passages with the public at large. This would lead both to persecution of the philosophers by the religious authorities and to a general weakening of faith as people came to doubt their understanding of religious doctrine and its practical principles. For some people it is sufficient to explain how the world came into being by saying that God created it out of nothing. For other people who are perhaps more aware of some of the difficulties of making sense of such an idea when one bears in mind the arguments for the existence of prior matter and the eternity of the world a different form of argument will be necessary. This form is produced by Maimonides when he talks about divine creation being comprehensible even within an Aristotelian framework. It is worth noting, though, that this more sophisticated view imports theological difficulties if combined with the simplistic notion of God as just someone very powerful who brings the world into existence out of nothing. For one thing, Maimonides seems to imply that the notion of creation *ex nihilo* is no more certain than the idea of eternal existence of the world, which is an unnerving view on religious grounds. Secondly, whatever one might say about Maimonides' account of divine creation and knowledge, it clearly involves a very different deity than that to which religious language has accustomed most believers.

It might be thought that the argument produced here is all very well but does it tackle the important issues? Reines points out that Maimonides does talk about God in ways which describe him, in apparent contravention of one of the leading themes of the *Guide*. If this usage contradicts that theme, then we have given support to the idea of Maimonides' use of the literary device of contradiction both to hide and to reveal his real views at the same time and to different audiences. Yet Maimonides has an explanation for the different sorts of language which are used to address different types of audience that is independent of the use of contradiction. It is a familiar theme among the Islamic philosophers that it is no part of the philosopher's role to dismantle the simple belief of ordinary people. From Farabi to Averroes it is continually argued that different expressions must be used for different people, and the philosopher must argue his case without confusing or threatening general religious adherence. The point was not lost on them that Socrates was put to death for (partially) expressing himself in such clear terms that the general Athenian public felt their moral and religious beliefs challenged by him (*I*, p. 198: Farabi, *Alfarabi's philosophy of Plato and Aristotle* tr. and int. M. Mahdi (Ithaca, Cornell University Press, 1969), p. 66). Maimonides is quite clear that most people need highly figurative language to help them observe religious rules and understand the principles of their faith, and provided that that language does not lead them astray in their practice, there is nothing wrong with it. Ordinary believers may well require figurative and illustrative language to be able to relate emotionally to their religion, and that is why any religion which has claims to be generally accessible must import such a means of representation to get its message across.

The view which Maimonides is proffering is that there are many layers of understanding and awareness which represent a continuum of different levels of believers. The basis to the whole model is the pared-down notion of a deity who can only be described in negative terms. Although he is less censorious about descriptions in terms of divine actions than other sorts of predicates, it is clear that such description is far from perfect. It gives rise to the temptation to think of the deity as a craftsman with creation as his product, and this is again to import human imagery into a context where it is essentially inapplicable. But is the idea of a description of God as an unknowable subject even coherent? It might well be wondered what is left once we have done away with every divine attribute.

Maimonides tends to follow the approach of Avicenna on the relationship between essence and existence, and treats the latter as a predicate of the former (in marked contrast to the critique of this analysis by Averroes (*A*, pp. 104–116). If existence is a predicate like any other predicate, then once we have stripped the concept of God of all its predicates we are not even left with a God who exists. Clearly this is not Maimonides' view, but it might be an implication of his argument. Pressing this point would be to ignore, though, the very special way in which essence and existence are related in the concept of God on Maimonides' analysis. Existence is not just a quality which the deity might or might not possess – it is identical with its essence and a necessary aspect of that essence. We may not know what to define as part of God's essence given the unknow-ability of that essence, but there is at least one positive claim that we can make about it, and that is the claim that it is necessarily instantiated. This is not something we find out about through obser-vation or through combining a multiplicity of parts in a subject as we do with normal definitions. The essence of God is simple and unified, and it consists in his necessary existence. This form of existence is to be contrasted with what we understand by existence, which is entirely different because we are entirely different creatures – contingent rather than necessary beings.

Leo Strauss thinks that this position is 'entirely negative and even subversive. For the doctrine [of attributes] culminates in the assertion that we grasp of God only that he is and not what he is' ('How to begin', p. xlviii) Strauss is firmly of the view that 'the teaching that positive attributes of God are impossible . . . clearly contradicts the teaching of the law' ('How to begin', pp. xlviii-xlix). This appears to be a naïve interpretation. Maimonides argues on the contrary that 'he who claims that God has affirmative properties . . . has done away with his belief in the existence of the deity without being aware of it' (*GP* I, 60; 145). Such a simplistic view of the nature of God would imply for Maimonides a refusal to grasp the most essential characteristics of the deity of which we can be aware, namely, his total separateness and transcendence from what we regard as the content of our experience. The very best way in which we can relate to the idea of God is where we can hold it in our minds as an object of pure love and contemplation, and where we approach the deity with an attitude of disinterested love. We tend to attribute to God properties which we regard as

34

perfections of ourselves, but they are really with respect to God 'the highest degree of imperfection' (*GP* I, 26; 56). The best way of coming to know what God is and how he acts is to remain silent and emphasize his overwhelming distinctness from everything else in the universe.

It would seem at this stage that there is something to be said for the point which Strauss is making here, a point which has a long history in the Jewish community. It rather seems that there are two ways of coming to know God: a superior and an inferior way, with a variety of gradations along a continuum. Most believers naïvely regard the deity as someone rather like themselves, but more so, and as a result of their belief follow religious law. They are basing their actions on beliefs which they take literally to be true, and which on Maimonides' account thereby mislead them radically. On the other hand, there are the sophisticated believers, who know that it is a mistake to identify the deity with human characteristics and that the best way of understanding God is by at every stage refusing to regard him as like us. Within the tradition of *falsafa* this contrast between different ways of approaching God arises time and time again, and the means of resolution are similar within the tradition as a whole. They take this form. Any religion is designed to appeal to the widest group of people possible. It is the aim of religion to make available to everyone who is capable of accepting a very basic set of propositions an understanding of who they are and how they are to live. That is why figurative language is so important. Such language is designed to help people incapable for one reason or another of working out how to behave where their duty lies and what wider considerations bear upon their practice.

It might nonetheless seem as though there were two views of God, one which is appropriate and one which is false. The former view is limited to the philosophically skilled, while the latter is reserved for those members of the majority in the community who just try to obey religious law. Such a contrast would indeed be subversive of any religion, and not just Rabbinic Judaism. This contrast is not one which Maimonides would seek to construct. Rather, there are two routes to an appreciation of God's transcendence, one reserved for the more intellectually able and one available to everyone. Observance of religious law makes possible the majority's awareness of God's transcendence in a practical and experiential manner rather than intellectually. The network of law and its obligations, which are divinely set out, represent divine transcendence in an imaginative rather than conceptual manner, and enable most people to participate in the transcendence of God by following their moral and social obligations. They are assisted psychologically in their adherence to the law by their imaginative (and strictly speaking, misleading) notion of God as a personal and discussable individual. Even a slightly higher level of believer, the theologians, might be helped in their adherence to law by their identification of God with characteristics such as eternity, omniscience, and so on, as though this explained why the law has the form and rationale it possesses. Maimonides uncompromisingly dismisses the validity of even these abstract predicates by claiming that any such attribute when applied to God is equivalent to attributing a body to him (*GP* I, 50). But if this form of theological analysis makes it more likely for theologians to follow divine law, then he has no qualms about letting them use it, so long as it is not taken to represent a valid analysis of the essence of the deity.

It looks as though it does not matter what sort of beliefs we might have about God provided that they do not get in the way of our religious behaviour. After all, many of the kinds of belief which Maimonides apparently endorses for their pragmatic value he at the same time criticizes for their inappropriateness. For Maimonides there are two aspects to a particular belief, its truth and the way in which it can lead to certain kinds of action. To understand what a religious sentence really means is a considerable intellectual achievement which cannot be expected of most believers. Yet they can still grasp a version of that sentence and, through its ability to move them in certain directions, they can participate in its real meaning. After all, Maimonides argues:

> Know that all the practices of worship, such as reading the Torah, praying and carrying out other commandments, have as their sole aim training you to concern yourself with his commandments . . . as opposed to matters relating to this world. You should behave as if you were concerned with him . . . and not with whatever is other than him.

(GP III, 51; 622)

Carrying out one's religious obligations is a means of coming to have the appropriate relationship with the deity which is available to all believers. It is important to regard carrying out those obligations as part of a process and not the end of the process of understanding the nature of the deity. It is an error for me to regard God as someone like a father or king who may punish me should I break the rules which he has established, since this is to attribute him with human qualities. On the other hand, if my adherence to the law is made more likely through such an attitude then I should adopt it, because the more used I get over time to obeying divine law, the more will my character change to become less concerned with my own desires and petty interests and the more involved with the general rules of a devout lifestyle.

Why not just insist that people follow religious law for the right reasons from the start? An important aspect of the answer here is the nature of ritual and practice as training. God could have insisted that the Israelites ceased worshipping him through the medium of sacrificing animals, a practice which is clearly inappropriate for a deity who does not eat and drink, nor see and hear. Maimonides suggests that since the Israelites were used to animal sacrifice as an expression of divine service it would have been inappropriate to require them to abandon it. What is important is the state of mind which carrying out such practices produces, and if these are capable of bringing out to people the immense gap between the deity and his creation, and the awe and love they are to feel for him, then they will have performed their task adequately. Maimonides extends this illustration by suggesting that if a prophet were to come in his own day and inform the community of the necessity of abandoning the practice of prayer to a deity with whom we can have no relationship, and replace the ritual of prayer with individual meditation on God, this would be a recipe for disaster. Referring to the sacrifices and genuflection before images in temples he comments:

> His wisdom and his gracious plan, which is displayed in regard to all his creatures, did not require that he give us a law prescribing the rejection, abandonment and abolition of all these kinds of worship. For one could not then conceive the acceptance of [such a law], since people always like doing that to which they are used. At the time it would have been similar to a prophet in these times who, calling upon the people to worship God, would say: 'God has given you a law forbidding you to pray to him, to fast, to call upon him for help in misfortune. Your worship should consist solely in meditation without any works at all'.
>
> (*GP* III, 32; 526)

We shall come to see in subsequent chapters what Maimonides means precisely by 'meditation without any works'. What he brings out in this passage is his view of God acting in harmony with human nature and encouraging a slow development of progressively correct attitudes as opposed to a revolutionary change in human thinking. This is an appropriate model for Maimonides' view of the difficulties involved in bringing our thinking about God around to the condition in which it should operate. We have to work hard to achieve an understanding of how the deity can work his influence on the world without at the same time identifying him with a human creator, and much of the *Guide* deals with suggestions as to how we are to carry this project out.

3

Imagination and the objectivity of prophecy

The notion of imagination in the work of Maimonides is difficult to pin down, and yet is crucial in any evaluation of his theory of prophecy and the literal truth of scripture. Maimonides has often been interpreted as having argued that prophecy is merely an internal psychological process, like having a dream, where the question of a corresponding external reality does not arise. He does indeed claim that the difference between a dream and a prophecy is only a matter of degree, and suggests that wherever angels are mentioned in the Bible what is meant is really a description of an imaginative experience, rather than an historical event. Religious thinkers may question the linking of something as significant as prophecy in their religions to dreams (or even to the presence of angels) and they are concerned about the apparently open cheque which Maimonides provides for the transformation of literal biblical texts describing historical events into something else which is far more nebulous. Is it true, then, that Maimonides' account of prophecy is a radical departure from religious and philosophical orthodoxy with respect to scriptural analysis, and what is it about the notion of imagination which led him to make so much use of it in his work?

The first point to make about Maimonides' account of prophecy in his *Guide of the Perplexed* is that he seems to treat it as a natural phenomenon. He used Avicenna's model of how the world works, and this model is characterized by emanation. There is taken to be a continual flow of emanations from God transmitted through a variety of separate intelligences until the active intellect is reached, which in turn provides the forms for the lowest level of existence, our sublunary world (*I*, pp. 34–35). There is no obvious room in this model for individual acts of grace on particular occasions, but basically a continuing supply of grace which will be received by anyone who is an appropriate recipient. As Maimonides puts it, 'it is a natural thing: for everyone who according to his natural disposition is fit for prophecy . . . to become a prophet' (*GP* II, 32; 361).

What is this natural disposition in human beings which puts them in the appropriate state of being for prophecy? A necessary condition is a morally acceptable character, but this is clearly not sufficient. Intellectual ability is also required. The freely flowing grace which wanders around the universe (originating from the deity) perfects an individual's rational and imaginative abilities. Theoretical perfection results from the effect of this grace on the rational faculty, while practical perfection results from its effect upon the imagination. This latter means that the prophet can both devise rules of behaviour appropriate for morally acceptable conduct and at the same time communicate important and complex truths about the universe and morality to the generality of the religious community. Insofar as the ordinary run of prophets goes (i.e. excluding the very special case of Moses), God is only a remote cause of their acquisition of prophetical powers – the active intellect is the more immediate agent of change – and only works where the recipient has orientated himself through intellectual work and an ethical lifestyle to produce an appropriate receptacle for the divine overflow of grace which makes prophecy possible.

Why is imagination important in this description of prophecy? Wolfson has argued persuasively that Maimonides tends to use the concept of imagination fairly loosely to include a wide variety of the internal senses, but what is made possible by the imagination is the combination and separation of ideas ('Maimonides on the internal senses', pp. 441–67). We receive impressions from our five senses, and then we may reorganize those impressions in different ways, as when we link the present impression of hunger with the impression of the previous lack of breakfast. Although imagination clearly involves thought, it is generally taken in medieval philosophy to be a form of thought more closely related to sense perception and to action than to abstract thinking itself. This is largely explained by the different objects of imagination and reason. The former generally has as its object practical action, the sort of action made possible by the sense impressions received and then *used* in some way. When we use reason to consider abstract ideas, though, this thinking normally goes on with entirely theoretical considerations in view. Imaginative thought is closely related to the future, to what will happen in the future and how the imaginer will react to those events. A person may have a strong imagination which results in veridical dreams and accurate predictions about future events. Someone who has both a strong imagination and a strong intellect, together with appropriate moral and physical qualities, is a prophet. He will not only know what is going to happen, he will know why it is going to happen, and not just at an empirical level but with some deeper insight into its divine provenance and rationale. He will also possess appropriate skills in communicating that information to others, a practical and pictorial ability which clearly involves the ability to use imagination. Maimonides recognizes that there are different levels of attainment of imagination, intellect and prophecy, and enters into some detail on how different ingredients result in different imaginative and prophetic cocktails.

Let us look at the development of the notion of imagination in the *Guide*. In the first part he is rather rude about imagination, relating it sometimes to fancy and to problematic thinking, as in 'It is manifest that to imagine is a deficiency' (*GP* I, 47; 105), and frequently to people just getting things wrong because they stick to what they imagine to be the case rather than the truth itself which could be reached were they to use their reason adequately. He attacks the theologians, the *mutakallimūn*, for claiming that 'everything that may be imagined is an admissible notion for the intellect', in other words, that everything which is imaginable is possible (*GP* I, 73; 206). He moderates his charge a little further on when he accepts that they acknowledge the illegitimacy of some images – 'they are aware of it to a certain extent; they know it and call that which may be imagined while being at the same time impossible – as for instance God's being a body – a fantasy and a vain imagining' (*GP* I, 73; 211). Yet he goes on to ask how they know that they are entitled to rule out this image. Imagination will not rule it out:

> For the imagination apprehends only that which is individual and composite as a whole, as it is apprehended by the senses; or compounds things that in their existence are separate, combining one with another. . . . Thus, someone using his imagination imagines a human individual having a horse's head and wings and so on. This is what is called a thing invented and false, for

nothing existent corresponds to it at all. In its apprehension, imagination is in no way able to hold aloof from matter, even if it turns a form into the extreme of abstraction. For this reason there can be no critical examination in the imagination.

(*GP* I, 73; 209–10)

Maimonides is pointing to an important characteristic of imagination here, namely, that in imagining there is nothing with respect to which the imaginer can be said to be mistaken, for there is nothing outside the imagination which the imagination can use to compare the imaginative presentation. As Merleau-Ponty puts it, 'the imaginary has no depth, and does not respond to efforts to vary points of view' (*Phenomenology of Perception*, p. 323). If the *mutakallimūn* want to deny the acceptability of God having a body, how are they to do it? Is not imagination just up to us? As Wittgenstein puts it, 'images are subject to the will' (*Zettel*, p. 621). Imagination by itself has no ability to distinguish between true and false possibilities, since truth values are a function of propositions, which presuppose universal concepts and intellectual abstraction. By contrast, the imagination is irretrievably tied to individual sense impressions, which it may combine arbitrarily. The imagination can then picture what is not the case and what cannot be the case, while finding it impossible to imagine what is the case. He illustrates the latter by giving the example of two people both able to stand on opposite ends of the world facing each other, and two lines extending indefinitely, so constructed that though they approach each other they never meet (*GP* I, 73; 210). If we are to understand these propositions we must employ the intellect to classify things in terms of essential and accidental properties, in terms of the species and genus to which they belong. This knowledge, which alone is capable of determining the truth value of propositions, is knowledge of the universal characteristics of objects, while imagination concentrates upon the particular sense impressions it is given and moves them about as it wishes, with no reference to truth conditions. In the first part of the *Guide*, then, the view of imagination which emerges is hardly a very positive one.

In the second part of the *Guide* Maimonides goes even further when he claims that 'imagination . . . is also in true reality the evil impulse' (*GP* II, 12; 280). He is referring here to our tendency to use anthropomorphic language when trying to imagine how God or angels might bring about events in the world. But when he later comes to a detailed discussion of prophecy, imagination is represented in a different and far more favourable light. It is described as an entirely natural bodily faculty, which can be healthy (and so very receptive) and unhealthy (and very unreceptive). Unlike our intellectual or moral character it is impossible to acquire or improve through hard work or training in good works. One is either imaginative or one is not. Now, Maimonides makes the point that imagination is closely involved with the senses, and that it works best when the senses are fairly dormant. He adds 'it is then that a certain overflow overflows to this faculty according to its disposition, and it is the cause of veridical dreams. This same overflow is the cause of the prophecy' (*GP* II, 36; 370). Then he says, very surprisingly, 'there is only a difference in degree, not in kind' between such dreams and prophecy, citing a couple of Talmudic sayings which he thinks supports his view, but which are far from clear and have little if any demonstrative foundation. What Maimonides seems to have in mind here is that there is a similarity between the way in which people when asleep may formulate accurate representations of future events with the use of imagination so 'that it sees the thing as it were outside, and that the thing whose origin is due to it appears to have come to it by the way of external sensation' (*GP* II, 36; 370). It is important to grasp here that Maimonides is relating *veridical* dreams with prophecy, and there is something to be said for this comparison. Such dreams have the status of raw ingredients out of which the prophet constructs a product with significant religious content.

To be a prophet, then, the overflow reaches both the rational and the imaginative faculties, where the latter is perfected through its natural disposition. If only the rational faculty is reached, then the result is 'characteristic of the class of men of science engaged in speculation' (*GP* II, 37; 374). Maimonides' low opinion of politicians emerges when he describes them as people with a perfected imagination but nothing else. Such people are lumped together with soothsayers and dreamers of veridical dreams who may well think of themselves as prophets since they 'have – even while they are awake – extraordinary imaginings, dreams and amazed states' (*GP* II, 37; 374). Maimonides goes on to widen the range of people with veridical predictions even further when he claims 'Similarly the faculty of divination exists in all people, but varies in degree' (*GP*

II, 38; 376). What he means by this, though, is quite restricted, that some people (indeed, all people) can work their way from the present situation to some sort of accurate prediction of what will happen in the future. This leads him to describe in some detail the internal workings of prophecy. What happens when the overflow perfects both the imagination and the rational faculty is that the latter works out very quickly what is going to happen, while the imagination puts this information into the appropriate form so that it appears to be sensory data. Our reason runs through an argument process extremely quickly, without all the intermediary steps of premisses, inferences and evidence occurring to us, and then the imagination represents the result of this lightning exercise of reasoning in a figurative form which makes it comprehensible to us. Maimonides is using a notion here imported from the work of Avicenna, and ultimately Aristotle, namely, that the things in the world are cognizable by syllogistic reasoning which mirrors in some way the world's structure, and if we could master the major premisses of these syllogisms the structure of the world would become perspicuous to us. The prophet masters some of these and thus is able to relate some aspects of present reality to the future, since 'all things bear witness to one another and indicate one another (*GP* II, 38; 377 and *I*, pp. 111–13).

This description of prophecy and its distant but nonetheless significant link with accurate predictions emphasizes yet again the naturalness of being a prophet, of having the appropriate characteristics for that role. When Maimonides comes to discuss the meaning of terms used in scriptural descriptions of prophecy, this impression is strengthened. Referring to Daniel, he says that:

> The speech of the angel to him and his setting him upright, all this happened in a vision of prophecy. In a state such as this the senses too cease to function, and the overflow in question comes to the rational faculty and overflows from it to the imaginative faculty so that the latter becomes perfect and performs its function.
>
> (*GP* II, 41; 385)

When things happen through the agency of angels and when God is said to have spoken to someone, these events all take place 'in a dream or in a vision of prophecy' (*GP* II, 41; 386). Maimonides repeats this point several times, emphasizing that 'it should by no means occur to your thought that an angel can be seen or that the speech of an angel can be heard except in a vision of prophecy or in a dream of prophecy', to which he adds, rather threateningly for the literalist, 'You can draw inferences from what I have mentioned as to what remains of the things that I have not mentioned' (*GP* II, 42; 390). Sometimes these visions are taken to constitute parables in themselves which then require the imagination to sift through possible interpretations of equivocal terms and their denotations. Even where there is no direct reference to the presence of an angel or a vision or a dream when we come to passages in which God apparently spoke directly to people, we should understand that the reference to a dream or vision is implicit in such a passage (*GP* II, 46; 404). All such apparent communication requires some form of intermediation by the imaginative faculty (*GP* II, 45; 403) with the exception, of course, of the very special paradigmatic form of prophecy enjoyed by Moses. Indeed, Maimonides is rather sharp with people who interpret literally scriptural passages in which someone is ordered to do something by a divine source when he says that 'Only those weak in syllogistic reasoning fancy with regard to all this that the prophet tells that he was ordered to do certain things and hence did them' (*GP* II, 46; 405).

It seems clear that when Maimonides talks about angels existing, he is using a special sense of existence. Although he starts *GP* II, p. 6 with the positive statement that 'The fact that angels exist does not require that a proof deriving from the Law be brought forward. For the Torah has stated this in a number of passages' (pp. 261), he later comments:

> Accordingly, Midrash Qoheleth has the following text: When man sleeps, his soul speaks to the angel, and the angel to the cherub. Thereby they have stated plainly to him who understands and cognizes intellectually that the imaginative faculty is likewise called an angel and that the intellect is called a cherub.
>
> (pp. 264–5)

'Soul' is generally taken to mean 'common sense', the faculty which first receives the impressions of the five senses and passes them onto the imagination (the angel). Common sense provides the imagination with sense impressions, which are then passed on in the form of images to the intellect where they are transformed into intellectual concepts. Imagination is the obvious candidate for the role of mediating between the senses and the intellect, and is especially relevant for prophecy. Imagination converts any kind of representation, whether intellectual, sensory or emotional, into powerful symbols and vivid ideas which then relate very directly to the question of appropriate action. This transformation into symbols makes possible the subsequent activity of the creature involved. The prophet is concerned with the actions of his community, and with impelling those actions to take a particular form and aim for a certain end. At the same time he realizes that he must present his case in a form which will be effective in persuading people of the necessity and desirability of change, and this involves imagination too. Imagination is obliged to deal figuratively with its data, since it is a material faculty and cannot as such grasp the universal and the immaterial. Normally, imagination deals with fairly low-level material, concerned as we are with our everyday lives and proximate issues. When we are asleep, though, the imagination is free to work on material which leads to knowledge in some people of future events, while the prophet's imagination is so well developed that he can have this sort of knowledge, and more, in waking life, and it can seem to have similar experiential status as his normal sense data.

The prophet, then, receives in a vision a message of some kind, a private message, one which should not be taken to be available to all in the same way as it is available to him. Yet this message is also supposed to have objective validity, and to touch on extremely important aspects of religious life within a community. How objective can it be when we are told (i) to discount all ideas that angels actually exist or that prophets are really ordered to do things, (ii) that the experiences which the prophet has are his alone, generically related to dreams and come about only if he has a well-developed imagination, and (iii) becoming a prophet is to a degree a matter of nature rather than nurture, like having red hair? Add to all these points Maimonides' view that the absence of prophecy from long periods of Jewish life is not taken to have anything directly to do with God's wishes but rather with the exigencies of life in exile. The minds of the people who are constituted in the appropriate manner to receive the overflow are over-involved with contemporary practical difficulties of coping with the difficult times and their resulting debilitating effects upon the realization of intellectual perfection (*GP* II, 36; 373).

It is hardly surprising that commentators should have taken this collection of views as very challenging to the intellectual bases of the interpretation of scripture and religion. If we look briefly at the criticisms of one of Maimonides' acutest critics, Isaac Abrabanel, we find a very clear set of arguments that the former's theory of prophecy is misguided. The correct position is that prophecy is not a natural event, but a miracle divinely brought about. God can grant prophecy to whomever he wishes, and intellectual, imaginative, and physical perfection is not required (although moral qualities still are). Prophets other than Moses do not have to employ their imagination when prophesying – they can attain prophecy by the use of their intellects alone. Dreams and prophecy are not part of the same species at all, and the rabbinic passages which Maimonides quotes should be taken as claims of the large differences between prophecy and dreams, not their similarity. In short, the difference between Maimonides and what might be thought of as the 'standard' religious view is well put by Abrabanel in his use of the image of the prophet's mind being like a mirror reflecting a divine message, where 'far be it from God to make his prophets similar to fools, madmen, and the sick by the impression of images upon their eyes that do not exist outside the mind' (Reines, *Maimonides and Abrabanel on Prophecy*, p. 123). What is reflected in the mirror of the mind must be, in the case of prophecy, something sent by God which is true, objective and real, not the result of someone's imagination or something like the train of events which takes place in a dream.

Let us look in some more detail at this question of the objectivity of prophecy in Maimonides's view. His predecessor Avicenna discussed this problem and rather ambiguously refers to angels as existing in both an absolute sense and relatively to us, but from his account it seems clear that what is meant is that the prophetic message is 'real' but the angelic appearance is just that: an impression which helps the recipient understand the message. A sympathetic interpretation of Maimonides is provided by Hillel of Verona, who discusses Jacob's struggle with the angel thus:

There is no doubt whatever that the struggle was literally real . . . I will never believe though that the angel was a body with joints and arms, but it happened like this: the angel, by means of a spiritual divine power, created in the air surrounding Jacob motions of thrust and pressure, through which the particles of air were violently moved and by their movement forced the body of Jacob, by pressing and coercing it as in the thrust of wrestling ... to move to and fro ... But the angel himself appeared to him, in truth, only in a 'prophetical vision' ... Thus the story of this event is literally true, as the real happenings were combined with the prophetical vision.

(Teicher, 'Christian Theology', p. 73)

This interpretation of Jacob's confrontation with the angel as a form of 'shadow wrestling' no doubt comes nearer to the literal meaning of the biblical text than Maimonides' view, yet remains basically unsatisfactory. Objectivity is based on the distinction between appearance and reality. To say that it is an objective matter whether or not a speaker's statement is true is to maintain that there is a clear difference between the claim's merely seeming to be true to the speaker, and its actually being the case. Maimonides' description of prophecy does not appear to leave room for objectivity with respect to the descriptive content of the prophetic utterance as these occur in scriptural passages.

Perhaps we can get clearer on the ontological status of the objects of prophetic imagination in Maimonides' account by looking at one of its sources, the discussion which Aristotle provides of *phantasia*, which has some meanings which incorporate the notion of imagination, and others which do not. For our purpose here it will not be too misleading to look at Aristotle's use of this term where it comes close to imagination. Aristotle links dreams with imagination, and yet they quite evidently differ from the latter in terms both of not being subject to the will and of not being emotionally detached from the nature of the experience undergone. When we dream we may well be terrified of the experiences we confront, whereas if we imagine being in a terrifying situation we might manage to remain detached from its emotional features. In addition, we can summon up imaginative experiences more-or-less at will, while dreams are not in this way under our control. Malcolm Schofield argues persuasively that what links dreams and imagination is the seeing of aspects. Aristotle's view of what happens in dreams is that something looks like something else, due to some small resemblance which it bears to that other thing. This represents a form of seeing as where one is 'forced' to see particular aspects at certain times, the sort of case in which one says something like 'I cannot help seeing x as y'. This is particularly the case when through some physical or mental disorder the aspects which arise are not under our control, but come about through a causal process. This is precisely the situation in the description which Aristotle and Maimonides give of veridical dreams; they occur apparently quite arbitrarily to certain people. The fact that the people who have such dreams are far from being the best and wisest led Aristotle to doubt that the source of such dreams was divine (*De divinatione per somnum* I, 462b 19–24).

As with Aristotle, Maimonides argues that the nature of individual minds has something to do with the ability to 'pick up' veridical dreams, and he adds that their external sources lie in the movements of the spheres which have an effect upon consciousnesses that are tuned into them. All this means is that some people are able to work out partially, in most part intuitively and without consciously thinking about it, how the world will change and develop over a period. They then grasp the future course of events, perhaps in the form of a dream which takes place when they are not concerned with more pressing matters. So when Maimonides relates prophecy to dreams this is not in itself to disparage the status of prophecy, but to point out that both phenomena involve the seeing of aspects and the reception of experiences which, unlike most imagination, is not under the control of the people involved. The dreams Maimonides compares with prophecy are not haphazard phenomena but controlled and directed reports of future events which mirror to a degree the way in which the world is transformed from one stage to another. They should not be compared with the ravings of fools and lunatics.

But even if this account of veridical dreams holds water, the question of the objectivity of the prophetic reports remains. It may be acceptable to anchor prophecy in the solid metaphysical foundations of the celestial spheres and the active intellect which together with the prophet's own faculties participate directly in the construction of prophetic knowledge. Of course, many people would feel distinctly unhappy about this model of prophetic causation, and the way in which Maimonides presents this process as a natural phenomenon, over which God appears to have no more than nominal control, yet these are not objections against the actual objectivity of the prophetic message. Imagination is only a necessary condition of the attainment of prophecy, and far from being sufficient. The prophet is not taken to be a creative, quasi-poetic genius intent on producing aesthetic objects rather than reporting historical truth. Maimonides makes it clear that the imagination only comes into operation after the intellect has been affected by the overflow of the active intellect, and since it deals with particular images rather than universal concepts, it is crucially involved in the accurate prediction of future individual events by producing the minor premisses in a large number of syllogistic reasonings. In addition, as we have seen, imagination is also involved in the communication of the prophecy to the community by enabling the prophet to explain his knowledge in the most comprehensible and persuasive manner.

This could all be accepted and yet still the challenge remains to explain how we can regard the prophetic message as objective when we are told by Maimonides that much of this message is in the form of parables, with ambiguous images and equivocal language, with a literal meaning which appears to be very different from its symbolic meaning. When we are told that angels visited Lot and told him to escape from Sodom with his wife, are we being told something which is literally true? Or is this merely a story designed to be believed by the unsophisticated masses, and seen behind by the intellectual élite for what it is, a parable indicating something else? We can clarify these questions by returning to Aristotle's discussion of the concept of imagination. One of the points which he makes about this concept is that it seems to hover between perception and thinking. He argues that:

> It is not possible to think without imagining. For the same effect occurs in thinking as in drawing a diagram. For in the latter case, though we do not make any use of the fact that the size of the triangle is determinate, we nonetheless draw it with a determinate size. And similarly someone who is thinking, even if he is not thinking of something with a size, places something with a size before his eyes, but thinks of it not as having a size.
>
> (*De memoria* I, 449b 31–450a 5)

The process of thinking is distinct from imagination, but it cannot go on without imagination. Aristotle's point here is that what one engages in thinking about and what one imagines in so thinking may be distinct in this sense. If someone wishes to make a point about triangles, she may well make a point about a particular triangle, but in imagining the particular triangle she is not (just) thinking about that triangle, but about all triangles. The prophetic vision has a certain content which enables us to work towards a more general point; it may be a fantasy and yet at the same time not illusory nor deceptive, but a symbolic representation of reality (*I*, pp. 182–5). The story of Sodom, then, may be in its entirety a prophetic fantasy experienced by Abraham. It is irrelevant to ask about the details of the story since its purpose is not to give an historical analysis of a factual event, but to present an allegory in which the wickedness of Sodom and the virtue of Lot are contrasted. If we return to Aristotle's point about imagination, what we think about and what we imagine in so thinking may be distinct. We are to think about a contrast between wickedness and virtue, and we have to imagine this within a particular narrative framework. The point of talking about a particular triangle is not to talk about that particular triangle, but about something else, viz. all triangles. The point of talking about Lot and Sodom is not to talk about a particular event, but about something else, the contrast between virtue and vice. The question of the historical accuracy of the report of that event, like the question of whether there actually is a triangle of the same size as the one imagined, is just irrelevant. It does not arise.

The only objectivity which we can talk about here is the objectivity of the relationship between the parable and its implications, between how we think of a state of affairs and the state of affairs which as a consequence is made comprehensible to us. Objectivity thus lies in the way in which what we imagine implies what we can think, and in what causally led to that exercise of imagination. If we think in this way about the use which Maimonides makes of the notions of the imagination and prophecy (and again, it must be emphasized, it is non-Mosaic prophecy which is at issue here), then we can defuse much of the literalist critique and regard the question 'But did it really happen?' as besides the point.

How reasonable is this view of Maimonides which presents prophecy as the preserve of imagination and yet at the same time objective? We should recall that he claims that there is only a difference in degree and not in kind between veridical dreams and prophecy, that everyone can predict the future to some extent and that there are plenty of indicators in the natural world as to how things are going to turn out. The prophet is a person who is very good at understanding these indicators and connecting one fact with another future fact, and he is equally skilled at presenting a story to the public as a whole which moves people to act and believe in certain ways. Maimonides is pointing here to a type of reasoning with which we are all familiar. Some people are very good at examining the evidence which confronts them and going on to make predictions of some accuracy about the future. These are the people who (consistently) make money on the Stock Exchange. Calling them imaginative is highly appropriate, since they are able to imagine future consequences of present actions which are obscure to those of equal or indeed greater intelligence but of less imagination. The comparison with veridical dreams is a useful idea, since in such dreams the images in one's mind are shuffled about in apparently arbitrary and confusing ways, but with some purpose in allowing us to try out a range of possibilities and alternatives which is not possible while we are awake. When awake our concerns are with the practical considerations which dominate our lives, and our imagination is restricted to topics which concern us more closely and immediately. Yet dreaming (and even day-dreaming) breaks temporarily the connection between our everyday ideas and the events which most urgently press upon us, and permits us to try out a whole range of ideas and pictures which have no conceivable bearing on the way things really are now.

Maimonides is quite right in thinking that there is a possible link between dreaming and prophecy, given his naturalistic view of the world. We may appear to have haphazard experiences during our dreaming, but these arise out of our experience of the world and display our fears and aspirations, our concerns and hopes. They are thus quite clearly connected with our particular points of view, and although they are not under our conscious control, they clearly contribute to our present and future decisions and projects. For example, there may be a person for whom we have a considerable liking, and yet we may have a dream about him or her which brings to the surface the possibility that that person is antagonistic towards us. Some aspect of his or her behaviour may have affected us at some level of awareness and may only arise when we are asleep and exploring the whole gamut of suspected and imagined enemies. If that impression proves to be correct, then the dream is generically similar to prophecy, since it tells us in vivid and persuasive language and imagery how we should act.

For Maimonides everything in the world relates to everything else. The sublunar world is controlled by regular and accessible laws. It is possible in principle to understand completely the connection between one phenomenon and the entire system of other phenomena in the universe which is available to us. This is why prophecy and its miraculous nature must be identified with natural processes. If divine intervention in a personal mode could interfere with the way in which the world was organized, there would fail to be regular and lawlike connections between phenomena. Maimonides follows Avicenna in viewing the world as a complex but basically comprehensible system of necessary laws, and someone of sufficient intellectual power should be able to understand that system, using that understanding to work out what will happen in the future. One way in which we might become clearer on the reasoning involved here will be to look at the equivalence which Maimonides claims holds between different views of prophecy and on the creation of the world. Right at the start of the long section during which he discusses prophecy he asserts that 'The opinions of people concerning prophecy are like their opinions concerning the eternity of the world, or its creation in time' (*GP* II, 32). This claim is subsequently played down when he adds 'I mean by this that just as people . . . have . . . three opinions concerning the eternity of the world or its creation in time, so are there also three opinions concerning prophecy' (*GP* II, 32). Very few commentators accept this disclaimer, though, and there is general consensus that Maimonides means something important by the comparison. Of course, there is no reason why we should accept such a consensus, but it is worth exploring the reasoning behind it to see if it throws light on the natural interpretation of prophecy.

These are the three views on the creation of the world:

1c. The . . . opinion . . . of all who believe in the Law of Moses . . . that the world as a whole . . . after having been purely and absolutely nonexistent . . . through [divine] will . . . [was] brought into existence out of nothing.

2c. The . . . opinion of . . . [Plato] . . . that there exists a certain matter that is eternal as the deity is eternal. . . . He is the cause of its existence . . . He sometimes forms out of it a heaven and an earth, and sometimes he forms out of it something else.

3c.   The . . . opinion . . . of Aristotle, his followers and the commentators of his books . . . He thinks that this being as a
whole, such as it is, has never ceased to be and will never
do so; that the permanent thing not subject to generation
and corruption, namely, the heaven, also does not come
to an end . . . and . . . the thing subject to generation and
corruption, namely, that which is beneath the sphere of the
moon, does not come to an end.

(*GP* II, 13; 281–4)

These are compared with three views on prophecy. On the first
view, prophecy is an event brought about through the direct intervention of God in the world:

1p.   The first opinion – that of the majority of the pagans who
accept prophecy as true and also believed by some of the
common people professing our Law – is that God . . .
chooses whom he wishes from among men, [and] turns him
into a prophet. . . . According to them it makes no difference
whether this individual is a man of knowledge or ignorant,
old or young. However, they also demand as a condition
his having a . . . sound morality.

2p.   The second opinion is that of the philosophers. It affirms
that prophecy is a certain perfection in the nature of
man . . . When, in the case of a superior individual who is
perfect with respect to his rational and moral faculties, his
imaginative faculty is in its most perfect state and when he
has been prepared . . . he will necessarily become a prophet,
in that it is a perfection which belongs to us by nature.
According to this opinion it is not possible that an individual
should be fit for prophecy and prepared for it and not
become a prophet.

3p.   The third opinion is the opinion of our Law and the foundation of our doctrine. It is identical with the philosophic
opinion except in one thing. For we believe that it may
happen that one who is fit for prophecy and prepared for
it should not become a prophet due to the divine will. To
my mind this is like all the miracles and takes the same
course as they. For it is a natural thing that everyone who
according to his natural disposition is fit for prophecy and

54

who has been trained in his education and study should become a prophet. He who is prevented from it is like him who has been prevented, like Jereboam, from moving his hand, or, like the King of Aram's army going to seek out Elisha, from seeing.

(*GP* II, 32; 360–1)

What comes over clearly in these formulations is Maimonides' firm belief in the naturalness of prophecy. It is a state which we can reach by dint of the sorts of creatures we are by bringing to actuality a potential perfection, rather like swimming fifty metres. The intervention of God is required not at all for this natural process to take place. The examples he gives emphasize this point, since they refer to the miraculous prevention of a potentiality reaching its actualization. It is natural to see and to move, and only a supernatural power can interfere with these possibilities when nothing natural stands in their way. Similarly, the achievement of prophecy when a person is fit to receive it and is appropriately prepared is a natural event which can only be prevented by supernatural and miraculous intervention. A number of puzzles arise as a result of Maimonides' surprising assertions. For one thing, the view which he identifies as the official religious line is completely bereft of any support in the theological literature. It seems to be an uneasy compromise between a full-blooded religious and a philosophical view, and most commentators have invoked here the seventh cause of contradiction which Maimonides mentions in his Introduction:

In speaking about very obscure matters it is necessary to conceal some parts and to disclose others. Sometimes in the case of certain dicta this necessity requires that the discussion proceed on the basis of a certain premise, whereas in another place necessity requires that the discussion proceed on the basis of another premise contradicting the first one. In such cases the vulgar must in no way be aware of the contradiction; the author accordingly uses some device to conceal it by all means.

(*GP* Int; 18)

As might be imagined, this seventh cause of contradiction is produced like a rabbit from a magician's hat whenever difficulties arise in reconciling different assertions in the *Guide*. The implication here would be that Maimonides really adhered to the philosophical view but wanted to avoid shocking the more credulous of his readers, and so presented the third view as a sop to their lack of sophistication and their need for the notion of an active and interventionist deity.

Before we adopt what I regard as a rather desperate strategy here and drag out the poor seventh cause of contradiction yet again, let us see whether we can make reasonable sense of what Maimonides actually says. There are aspects of the philosophical view which accord quite neatly with accepted religious descriptions of prophecy. For example, the idea that before one can become a prophet one must prepare oneself adequately and develop to their fullest degree moral and intellectual virtues is surely appropriate from a religious point of view. Similarly, the insistence upon the possibility of divine action blocking what would otherwise be inevitable follows from the notion of God. The connection between this idea and the nature of the creation of the world is not difficult to fathom, either. Maimonides claims 'Know that with a belief in the creation of the world in time, all the miracles become possible' (*GP* II, 25; 329). If Aristotle's account of the creation of the world is correct, then the phenomenon of prophecy exists within the context of a necessary and eternal system of nature which makes inevitable the attainment of prophecy once the necessary and sufficient conditions are realized. The view which is ascribed to Plato would base prophecy upon nothing but the will of the deity, since the eventual corruption of the world would take with it any possibility of causal necessity. The third opinion seems quite feasible, then, as the view in accordance with the Law since it combines the philosophical account of the necessary structure of sublunar reality with the possibility of a God who can interrupt the way in which things behave.

How acceptable is this argument apparently produced by Maimonides? He clearly tries to combine the account of the natural world provided by Aristotle with the addition of a God who can alter and interfere in that world. Creation out of nothing is important since it would be inconceivable that such an active God could have his hands tied as it were by the nature of the material he was employing. He is rather in the position of the central heating engineer who constructs his own central heating system out of materials which he himself has created, and which he then sets by thermostat to perform in a certain way. The mechanism operates by itself quite acceptably, but it is always possible for the engineer to override the controls and alter the timing or temperature. An objection which might arise here is that this sort of approach runs counter to the very view of the order of the world upon which Maimonides bases his account of prophecy. Prophets, like other intellectually advanced individuals, can perceive connections and regularities in the structure of the world such that they are able to make accurate predictions of future events. Were the world to have the form it does because of an arbitrary arrangement at the beck and call of a creator, how could such regularity and connectedness be established and utilized by prophets? The answer is that although God could interfere to change the structure of the world, he never does:

> Though all miracles change the nature of some individual being, God does not change at all the nature of human individuals by means of miracles. . . . We do not say that this is the case because we believe that the alteration of the nature of any human being is difficult for him. . . . Rather it is possible and quite within his capacity, but according to the foundations of the Law of the Torah he has never willed to do it and never will.
>
> (*GP* III, 32; 529)

This seems to establish the third position on prophecy (3p) and the first on creation (1c) as Maimonides' own views. We shall look at the issue of creation later, but for the moment it also seems to present an acceptable view of the nature of prophecy in a universe which has room for an active and purposive deity.

But we cannot leave the issue in this uncomplicated state. It seems that Maimonides argues that God could alter the natural order in the world, but never does. This assertion would contradict the principle of plenitude, the principle that something which is possible has already happened or will happen at some time (*I*, pp. 32–7). This principle was first outlined by Aristotle and was adopted by most of the philosophers in the Islamic world, Jewish as well as Muslim. It is based upon the idea that 'It is not allowable that it is true to say "this is possible, but it will not be" ' (*Metaphysics*, 1074b 3). This idea was taken up by Averroes and converted into the argument that a possibility which was never actualized should be contrasted with a real possibility, which at some point is realized (*A*, pp. 112–13). The Peripatetic philosophers tended to extend the principle to everything which exists, thus introducing a great deal of necessity into the everyday world of generation and corruption, but Aristotle and Maimonides are careful to limit its application to eternal things like species. For Aristotle to claim that 'In everlasting things, there is no difference between being possible and being the case' (*Physics*, 293b 30) seems quite acceptable, since if something is eternal one would expect it to realize every potentiality which applies to it, given that there is no barrier in terms of time to prevent this taking place. In a letter to Samuel ibn Tibbon Maimonides explains the issue thus:

> When a species is said to be possible, it is necessary that it exists in reality in certain individuals of this species, for if it never existed in any individual, it would be impossible for the species, and what right would one have for saying that it is possible? If, for example, we say that writing is a thing possible for the human race, it is necessary then that there are people who write at a certain time, for if one believed that there is never any man who writes, that would be saying that writing is impossible for the human race. It is not the same when possibility is applied to individuals, for if we say that it is possible that this child writes or does not write, it does not follow from this possibility that the child must necessarily write at one particular moment. Therefore, the claim that a species is possible is not, strictly speaking, to place the species in the category of possibility but rather to claim that it is in some ways necessary.
>
> (Munk, *Le guide des Égares*, p. 39)

The point that Maimonides is making here is that if it is really possible for something to happen, and if there is no limit in terms of time in force, then it must at some time take place. He makes it clear that if there is the possibility of the highest degree of human perfection that is natural to our species then it must be realized in at least one individual, in this case Moses (*GP* II, 32). It would also seem to be the case that if it is possible for God to interfere with nature then he would at some point instantiate that possibility.

This difficulty might be easy to dissipate. The initial creation of the world in time could be seen as the one instance in which God's power to intervene in natural processes was actualized. It might seem a bit strange to interpret the setting up of the system of natural processes as an intervention, but presumably the idea is that the setting up of the natural system is an intervention in time. We should remember here that we are not to think of the creation of the world or divine intervention as an arbitrary event on a par with our creation of a work of art or a machine. Such creation has a purpose for which it is intended and we can more-or-less follow what went into its creation and how it was done. The creation of the world and the nature of divine intervention in nature emerge out of the divine essence in a manner which we cannot conceive. The only way in which we can derive any idea of what that essence is involves observing God's actions, namely, the natural world.

One of the most interesting and unusual arguments which Maimonides presents on prophecy relates to the prophecy of Moses. This is taken to be very different from ordinary prophecy, and indeed is unique. Moses received prophecy in an entirely different way from other people, in that it was an utterly intellectual experience. For every other prophet the revelation arrived through an angel, by which he means that it employed imagination (*GP* II, 34; 367: II, 36; 373), but Moses received the prophetic revelation without any intermediary, when completely awake and at will, and without physical or mental disequilibrium. In fact, the distinction between Mosaic prophecy and ordinary prophecy is so great that 'to my mind the term prophet used with reference to Moses and to the others is amphibolous' (*GP* II, 36; 373) by which he means a term 'predicated of two things between which there is a likeness in respect to some notion, which notion is an accident attached to both of them and not a constituent element of the essence of each one of them' (*GP* I, 56; 131). In the ordinary account of prophecy we are told that there is an overflow from the active intellect which reaches the imagination after first being received by the rational faculty. Moses misses out the use of the imagination entirely, and only his intellectual ability is required for prophecy. Essentially, then, Moses is not a prophet in the sense that all the commonplace and everyday prophets are.

Moses does not require imagination because his intellectual abilities are so strong and what he has 'apprehended . . . has not been apprehended by anyone before him nor will it be apprehended by anyone after him' (*GP* I, 54; 123), Maimonides argues that there are three levels of prophecy, the lowest being entirely imaginative (as in veridical dreams and lucky guesses), the next being a mixture of intellectual and imaginative, and the very highest Mosaic form being entirely intellectual. This last type of prophecy requires as complete a subjugation of the physical desires and inclinations as it is possible to conceive of a human being accomplishing, so that the entire direction of the mind is on rational and metaphysical issues. Although the language which Maimonides uses in describing the uniqueness of Moses' prophecy makes him out to be almost a spiritual being, there is no doubt that only God can know 'the true reality, the nature, the substance, the form, the motions, and the causes of the heavens' (*GP* II, 24; 327). Moses may be the most perfect of humans when it comes to apprehending God, but even he is limited in his awareness and understanding of the divine qualities. This is due to his physical nature which necessarily interferes with the amount of time he can spend contemplating purely rational topics. When Moses was upset by events going on around him he was unable to prophesy, and this was because he was unable to direct his attention sufficiently strongly towards matters of an entirely intellectual nature.

One of the interesting questions which arises here is that if attention to non-rational issues interfered with Moses' prophecy, how could he combine his role as a prophet of extraordinary power with his political role as the leader of the community and legislator? The importance of imagination for the normal run of prophet is that it enables him to transfer his revelation in a mode acceptable and comprehensible to the masses in the community. It shows them how to use appropriate language to move the unsophisticated believer in the right direction, which a purely intellectual grasp of the issue could not do. This is very much a commonplace in discussions of prophecy within Islamic philosophy, that the use of imagination is vitally important as a political tool in translating the purely rational judgment concerning the right behaviour of the individual and the community into a form of words and ideas which everyone can grasp and accept (*A*, pp. 123–4). Divine law is both effective on the level of practical communication with ordinary human beings and urges them onto greater intellectual effort. This dual role of law comes out nicely in Maimonides' famous assertion that:

If you find a law all of whose ordinances are due to attention being paid . . . to the soundness of the circumstances pertaining to the body and also to the soundness of the belief . . . and that desires to make man wise . . . you must know that this guidance comes from him, may he be exalted, and that this law is divine.

(*GP* II, 40; 384)

The unique role which Moses plays is as the supreme legislator.

Why is Moses such an important figure for Maimonides? It was Moses who established the Jews as a political entity, and prophets before him had no such entity to address, while those who followed him were limited in asking the community to adhere to the Mosaic law. Moses did not just provide a number of prophetic utterances relating to legislation, he established the legislation in the first place, and the legislation defined the community. He is the only example of such a prophet, and no-one will appear in the future to abrogate his prophecy (*GP* II, 39; 416). We can see more clearly why such a strong distinction is drawn between the prophecy of Moses and the rest. His prophecy is specifically political, while other forms are dependent upon that political construction of a community and its laws. That is why Maimonides refers to the relationship between Mosaic and ordinary prophecy as amphibolous. A similar relationship holds between God's knowledge and human knowledge in the works of most of the Islamic philosophers, with the assertion that God's knowledge makes possible our knowledge since it provides the principles which underlie our way of knowing. We can know because God has established a particular organization of the world and created creatures with perceptive faculties, and while it is permissible to talk of his knowing at the same time as we talk of our knowing, it is important to realize that the sorts of knowledge at issue here are very different. They are very different, and at the same time they are to a degree similar, in that one form of knowledge makes possible another form.(Maimonides did not, of course, accept this formulation of the relationship between divine and human attributes.) This is precisely what he means here by calling prophecy amphibolous when used to describe Mosaic and ordinary prophecy.

An important distinction seems to arise between Moses and the rest of the prophets in the way in which they receive divine revelation. For the latter imagination is an important tool which permits them to impress the masses with the force of the word of God. Yet we are told that Moses received prophecy without any mediation from imagination, by using reason alone. How was it possible for him to formulate his prophecy into imaginative and forceful language which would appeal to the community at large? There can be no doubt that the law of Moses does not approach the truth directly but works slowly to change the thinking and practice of the community, combining rules which point to the real intellectual nature of human happiness with others which relate to more immediately attractive and accessible forms of happiness. It would obviously be a defect in the law if it did not appeal to the community at large, and there should be something in every law which makes it easy to comprehend why it should be followed. In other words, law should contain at least two elements, one which is rational and which embodies its purpose, and one which is persuasive and is designed to make its performance attractive generally. Now, from the accounts of Moses as a prophet we might be surprised to find that he can cope with the construction of both parts of the law. His intellect draws its inspiration directly from the principles embodied in the active intellect, and does not require the dreams, visions, metaphors and poetic language of the imagination. While 'We are like someone in a very dark night over whom lightning flashes time and time again. Among us there is one for whom the lightning flashes time and time again, so that he is always, as it were, in unceasing light. Thus night appears to him as day' (*GP* Int; 7), the inhabitants of the dark require language which they can understand if they are to accept the law provided by the prophet Moses who is generally aware of the true nature of reality, insofar as a human being can be. We need exactly the images, metaphors, poetry and visions to move us to understand as far as we can where our duty lies and how we should behave. How is a prophet of the purity of Moses able to provide us with this sort of persuasive material?

The answer seems to be that he did not need to, since his prophecy concerned matters which could be apprehended by the use of reason and the ordinary evidence of the senses alone. Moses told the Israelites at Mount Sinai:

This great gathering that you have seen has taken place only in order that you acquire certitude through sight, so that if, in order to make publicly known the extent of your faith, the Lord your God tried you out with a false prophet who would call upon you to demolish what you have heard, you should remain firm and keep your feet from stumbling. For if I had come to you as a prophet, as you had thought, and I had said to you what had been said to me without your hearing it for yourselves, it would have been possible for you to fancy that what is told by another is true even if that other had come to you with something contradicting what has been made known to you; this is what could have happened if you had not heard it at this gathering.

(*GP* III, 24; 500)

The Israelites had proof of the divine nature of the Law by hearing themselves the voice of God, albeit mediated in the form of natural phenomena, at Mount Sinai, and did not have to rely upon the revelation transmitted to Moses. For this reason the role of Moses is so crucial – he established the Law on a sure and indubitable foundation. Future generations are supposed to refer to the evidence which their ancestors had on that occasion of the divine origin of the Law. Lesser varieties of prophets use their imaginative skill to make the Law and its content appropriate and relevant to the particular conditions which exist in a given time for a certain community, and the way in which they go about their task is not to be compared with the way in which the Law is established in the first place. After all, one might query the validity of the miracles or stories produced by ordinary prophets and still remain faithful to the requirements of the Law, but a failure to accept the validity of the origins of the Law itself debars one from the community. Imagination provides an unsure attachment to the truth since the language and imagery employed may eventually come to be challenged, but nothing can challenge the evidence of our reason and our senses.

Maimonides is not arguing that imagination provides an inaccurate account of the truth, but that it directs our minds to the truth in a roundabout fashion. To take an example, he suggests that it would have been inappropriate to abolish sacrifices while the Temple was in existence, since this was a form of worship to which the community had become accustomed (*GP* III, 32). Once the Second Temple was destroyed and sacrifices came to be replaced by prayer and fasting, it was appropriate to seek another form of ritual. In another and even more enlightened time, he implies, prayer may be replaced by nothing more than meditation upon the works of God, which would involve the minimum use of images or persuasive language. A prophet has to work with the materials which are to hand, and he must relate his message to the current way of thinking in the community. The prophecy of Moses must not be considered on these lines, though, since there is nothing in it which can vary with variations in social and political conditions. The Law of Moses itself establishes the parameters within which that degree of alteration and development may take place. Once those parameters have been accepted one can see that 'the law, although it is not nature, enters into what is natural' (*GP* II, 40; 382). It seeks to change in a very gradual fashion what we regard as natural behaviour by producing conventions designed to alter, again very gradually, the way in which we think of ourselves and our God.

4

How did God create the world?

Maimonides clearly identifies the issue of the creation of the world as crucial to an understanding of God and his role in the universe. The view which he identifies as the orthodox Jewish view is that God existed at one time by himself and nothing else existed at all. God then decided to bring the world into being, and he was completely free to establish the sort of world he fancied. Nothing constrained him in his creation, no matter already existed which could only be shaped into particular forms, and no limitations existed which could force him to create in one way or another. The world was created out of nothing and nothing led to its creation except the will of its creator. The philosophers who were heavily influenced by Aristotle argued by contrast that the world has always existed and has the form it has out of necessity. These arguments take a variety of forms. In the first place, it is suggested that if the world did not exist, we could not even talk about the time during which its non-existence took place. This is because time is a function of motion, and if there exists nothing to move in the universe, we cannot really talk about time or 'before' and 'after'. God's putative creation of the world out of nothing could not then have taken place in time, since were it to have taken place it would have itself established time. How then can we say that first God waited, and then he created the world? What can be meant by thinking of a time before the creation of time? (*I*, pp. 41–4). Similarly, if the world could come to an end, we would have the problem of knowing how to talk about the time after the world finished, and time presumably finished with it.

Maimonides is also very critical of the version of Aristotelianism particularly clearly expressed by Avicenna which views the deity as a necessitating cause of necessitated phenomena. God is regarded as the only thing which is not brought about by something else, and the rest of the world is determined to have the form it has by the agency of a variety of causes. Ultimately the cause of everything is God, but the way in which creation unfolds is based upon a rationality which makes no reference to the will or decision of a personal God. Rather, a process is set in motion which necessarily unfolds in a particular way. From a religious point of view it might be thought that this model of the relationship between God and the world is unsatisfactory, and both Maimonides and Ghazali clearly felt dissatisfied with the theological implications of this view. Where was there room for the idea of a personal God intervening in human affairs, deciding what to do and observing the events in the world of generation and corruption? We have seen that Maimonides on one level disparages the need for the concept of this kind of personal God, but there is no doubt that in his comments on Aristotelianism concerning the issue of the creation of the world he sets out to rescue traditional religious notions from the grip of the philosophers. Whether he succeeds, and perhaps more importantly for most commentators, whether he even tried, remains to be seen.

Maimonides follows an interesting and complex strategy. He argues throughout that Aristotle presents the most cogent analyses of the nature of time, the world and the structure of natural events. And yet Aristotle is over-ambitious when he thinks he can conclude that the world is eternal. In fact, this is taken to be a claim more for the Aristotelians than for Aristotle himself; Aristotle is interpreted as having offered better arguments for eternity than his predecessors did for creation *ex nihilo* but he is taken to be aware of the non-demonstrative form of both his and their arguments on this topic. If this line of argument is successful, it will provide room for the creation *ex nihilo* concept in the sense that it will not rule out that concept, and one can appeal to prophecy in its support. Maimonides produces a proof of the creation in time notion and argues that the idea of divine purpose in the universe is incompatible with the idea of necessity (*GP* II, 15–24). Before we go on to look in closer detail at the structure of the argument here it is worth pointing out the similarities between this approach and that offered by Ghazali in his critique of Peripateticism on this and many other related topics. Ghazali too accepted Aristotelianism, at least for the sake of the argument, and then proceeded to show that even on Aristotelian premises the arguments of the philosophers fall down. When Ghazali points to the discrepancy between literal interpretations of the Koran and Peripatetic philosophy he does not just throw up his hands and say that this shows we can abandon philosophy as an impious activity. He argues that philosophy is representative of unbelief *and* at the time of fallacious reasoning (*I*, pp. 38–40: *A*, pp. 7–8). Maimonides is clearly more enthusiastic about philosophy than Ghazali, and yet he adopts what is basically the same strategy.

Why is it so important that Aristotle is not allowed to carry the argument on the eternity of the world? According to Maimonides:

> If we accept the eternity of the universe as taught by Aristotle, that everything in the universe is the result of fixed laws, that nature does not change and that there is nothing supernatural, we should necessarily be in opposition to the foundation of our religion, we should disbelieve all miracles and signs, and certainly reject all hopes and fear derived from scripture, unless miracles are to be explained figuratively.
>
> (*Treatise on resurrection*, p. 31)

Now, we have already seen that Maimonides does frequently interpret miracles figuratively, in the sense that they are natural events. Yet he does insist that if we can make sense of the sort of deity which is presupposed by scripture then there must be scope for intervention in the natural world by some power from without, whether or not that possibility is ever realized. Yet Maimonides accepts twenty-five of Aristotle's premises relating to the natural world and its structure, and one wonders how he can avoid the conclusion that the world is an entirely rule-governed system set in motion by a remote cause which is coeval with the universe. Surely Maimonides cannot intend to accept Aristotelianism as a whole with the addition of the proposition that God created the world after a period during which the world did not exist?

It might seem easy to combine both these propositions, but if we think seriously through the implications of the version of Aristotelianism which Maimonides accepted we can see the difficulties involved. Returning to his account of prophecy, he argued there that the world is such a connected environment that some people can know a great deal about the future by understanding what is going on at the moment, and such people are able to make accurate predictions about the future based upon what they know about the present. What is vital for such a possibility to be more than just a process of lucky guesses is an underlying order and regularity in natural processes. This order is taken to exist in nature itself, as opposed to being arbitrarily imposed on the world by its creator. If what went on was a function of divine will, in the same way that what I am doing now at the typewriter is a function of my will, then it would be difficult if not impossible to make accurate predictions about the future. Anything could happen, and the fact that anything could happen would do away with our present understanding of natural processes.

Maimonides appreciates that he cannot just apply the notion of creation *ex nihilo* to an Aristotelian model of the world, so he constructs a principle (which will be called 'Maimonides' Principle') that will allow him to be an Aristotelian at the sublunar level and a believer in God at the superlunar level. The Principle is 'No inference can be drawn in any respect from the nature of a thing after it has been generated, has attained its final state, and has achieved stability in its most perfect state, to the state of that thing while it moved toward being generated . . . nor . . . to its state before it begins to move thus' (*GP* II, 17; 295). When one looks at the Principle it seems rather persuasive, since it is difficult to draw inferences about the origins of things just by observing the thing itself. The ways in which things develop frequently gives one few grounds for being able to work backwards as it were from the fully developed object itself to the process which led up to it. On the other hand, the Principle seems rather weak, since in most cases we do know how a fetus becomes a human being, and how a tadpole becomes a frog. We know because of our science and powers of observation, and we can be satisfied that such knowledge claims are justified. Maimonides means more than this, though, since he wants to say that when we look at the world in its present state of development we cannot work out how it came into existence. One important argument he utilizes is that working back from the frog to the tadpole is entirely different from working back from the world to its creation. We can have experience of the former but not of the latter.

The point he is making is not just about relationships which we cannot establish empirically. Rather, he is suggesting that an entirely different form of reasoning is involved in talking about the creation of the world than is involved in discussing the creation of an aspect of it. According to him, Aristotle:

> said that the first matter is subject to neither generation nor corruption and began to draw inferences in favour of this thesis from the things subject to generation and corruption and to make clear that it was impossible that the first matter was generated. And this is correct. For we do not maintain that the first matter is generated as man is generated from the seed or that it decays as man decays into dust. But we maintain that God has brought it into existence from nothing and that after being brought into existence, it was as it is now – I mean everything is generated from it, and everything generated from it passes away into it; it does not exist devoid of form; generation and corruption terminate in it; it is not subject to generation as are the things generated from it, nor to corruption as are the things that decay into it, but is created from nothing. And its creator may at will make it entirely and absolutely nonexistent.
>
> (*GP* II, 17; 296)

Let us look at an example to establish Maimonides' argument. Suppose that I am sitting in my room and I suddenly see on my desk a stone which I have never seen before. I might say that it has come from nowhere, and the idea that it has suddenly come into existence seems on the face of it to be quite conceivable. But when we think about it we realize that if we are to speak of things coming into existence just like that, without any connection with anything already in existence or something preceding its existence, we are taking on board a very different conceptual scheme than that which we presently employ. Aristotle argues that when we talk about things changing we have in mind a continuing matter out of which the changes take place, and it is the presupposition of the existence of this matter which makes our talk about change possible. If just anything could happen regardless of its relationship to an underlying principle of matter, we should inhabit and experience a very different world, one in which it would be difficult to grasp an order and direction in things.

Maimonides' Principle seems to challenge this sort of analysis. He argues quite plausibly that the sort of explanation which is acceptable for an aspect of the world's behaviour is not necessarily acceptable for the behaviour of the world itself as a whole. Aristotle's analysis of natural events is taken to be valid in so far as it goes, but it goes awry if it seeks to explain the origination and the passing away of those events as a whole. As he says, 'we maintain that after it has become stable one cannot imagine that it should come into being as a whole and perish as a whole, as partial motions come into being and perish' (*GP* II, 17; 297). The interesting feature of Maimonides' approach here to this issue is that he seems so committed to the Aristotelian approach with the sole addition of the principle that Aristotelianism only works to explain the individual events in the world, not the world itself. There appears to be very little argument for his objections to the full-blooded Aristotelian claim, though, and this has led many commentators to argue that he was not sincere in his claim to have found a flaw in the Greek system. Maimonides' Principle is taken to be a fairly transparent attempt at declaring his orthodox belief in creation *ex nihilo* while alerting the philosophically inclined of his real adherence to Aristotle. It is true that he suggests 'that Aristotle's view is nearer to correctness than the opinions of those who disagree with him in so far as inferences are made from the nature of what exists' (*GP* II, 15: 292). But we need not share this esoteric interpretation to make sense of Maimonides' arguments, and as usual if we look for secret meanings we will miss interesting aspects of the reasoning.

In his discussion of creation Maimonides points to the equivocal meaning of the term *'adam* or non-existence. It can either mean 'nothing' or 'matter'. This has implications for our understanding of the expressions relating to creation in the Bible. Creation involves 'bringing into existence out of non-existence' (*GP* II, 30; 358) which is equivocal since *min 'adam* can mean 'out of nothing' or 'out of matter'. The former would apply to the ordinary religious view of creation while the latter would be compatible with Platonic and Aristotelian accounts. When Maimonides wants to be clear that he is talking about creation *ex nihilo* he uses two expressions, *ba'd al-'adam al-mahd al-mutlaq* (after pure and complete non-existence) and *la min shay* (not from something). He does not always want to present the notion of creation as being so clear and settled, and in his discussion of Genesis i:1 'God created the heaven and the earth' he purposefully uses the equivocal term *bara'* which can mean either out of something or out of nothing. He seems to accept as possible interpretations either the orthodox Jewish view that God created the world out of nothing and all at once when he wished to bring it about, or the idea that he used pre-existent matter, or even the idea that there is a continuous process of creation going on through which God remotely causes forms to structure the matter of the world and bring about the variety of objects of which we are aware. Why does Maimonides leave the issue so open? One suggestion is that he wished to indicate to philosophers his real view that the world was created out of something which is co-existent with God, while at the same time not challenging the simple faith and understanding of the majority of the community.

An argument for the esoteric interpretation is his apparent distrust of all the theological arguments for creation *ex nihilo* produced by the *kalām* (see *GP* I, 71). It looks as though he is too cautious to express his genuine adherence to a Platonic or Aristotelian view of the nature of creation in a clear and open fashion, and so he limits himself to presenting a variety of views with the explanation that the key terms he is using are equivocal. It will be remembered that Ghazali denounced this as a device for surreptitiously reducing the power and influence which God has over the world. But Maimonides might be taken to be arguing that on this issue caution is appropriate because it is impossible to be more definite. He does frequently suggest that 'With regard to this question – namely the eternity of the world or its temporal creation – no cogent demonstration can be reached and that it is a point before which the intellect stops' (*GP* I, 71; 180). He argues that both creation *ex nihilo* and the eternity of the world are possible views, and that neither view can be demonstrated with strict logical rigour.

Maimonides does produce a proof for creation *ex nihilo* which is a version of an argument popular among the *mutakallimūn*, the argument from particularization. This works on the principle that if Aristotelian physics were valid for the heavens as well as the sublunar world then the order in which the planets move would be different from what we know it actually is. There is a different celestial order, which implies the presence of an agent who establishes a particular structure in the system of the planets. We may not understand the purpose behind that structure, but what we should grasp is that its organization could not have come about through the action of material forces alone. In *GP* II, 22 he argues that the creation *ex nihilo* view is more likely than the eternity of the world thesis, but that neither can be definitely established on logical grounds. Before we come to explore this suggestion in more depth it is worth pointing out yet again that if Maimonides is really trying to hide a heterodox view he is not making a very good job of it. After all, if we take him at his word and accept that prophecy and miracles only make sense in a world which has been created by a God with purpose and choice, and if it is true that an eternal world would not be compatible with such a deity, then it is rather controversial to argue that the competing claims of eternity and creation are more-or-less equally acceptable. Of course, we might take the line that he really advocated Platonic ideas of an eternal matter which would make miracles conceivable and satisfy some philosophical problems concerning creation *ex nihilo*. If this was his view, why did he not frankly express it? Why should he have feared the consequences if he could have argued strongly for one of the alternative positions as an appropriate solution to the religious and philosophical problem of creation? Before we give in and seek an esoteric purpose to Maimonides' putative arguments, it might be profitable to see whether any philosophical interest exists in what he actually says.

An important contribution to his position here is developed in *GP* II, 24, a section in which he criticizes Ptolemaic theories of the heavens. He criticizes severely the sort of physics recommended by Ptolemaic astronomers for the sort of motion on the lines of eccentric and epicyclic models which they presuppose. His objections are based upon the apparent irreconcilability of Ptolemaic physics with Aristotelian scientific theory. Yet he is aware that if we look at planetary motion in the way that Ptolemaic theory suggests, we get good results. Referring to the principles of the epicycle and the eccentric, he asks:

> Is it any way possible that motion should be on the one hand circular, uniform and perfect, and that on the other hand the things that are observable should be observed in consequence of it, unless this be accounted for by making use of one of the two principles or of both of them?

> (*GP* II, 24; 325–6)

If Aristotelian physics does not yield good predictions when applied to the planets, but Ptolemaic physics, by contrast, does, the obvious line to take would be to reject the former and replace it with the latter. This is not Maimonides' conclusion. He takes the surprising direction of arguing that the astronomer is only interested in producing accurate results, not in describing the motion of the heavens:

> However, I have already explained to you by word of mouth that all this does not affect the astronomer. For his purpose is not to tell us in which way the spheres truly are, but to posit an astronomical system in which it would be possible for the motions to be circular and uniform and to correspond to what is apprehended through sight, regardless of whether or not things are thus in fact . . . However, regarding all that is in the heavens, man grasps nothing but a small measure of what is mathematical; and you know what is in it. I shall accordingly say in the manner of poetical preciousness: The heavens are the heavens of the Lord, but the earth hath He given to the sons of man. I mean thereby that the deity alone fully knows the true reality, the nature, the substance, the form, the motions and the causes of the heavens. But he has enabled man to have knowledge of what is beneath the heavens, for that is his world and his dwelling-place in which he has been placed and of which he is a part. This is the truth. For it is impossible for us to accede to the points starting from which conclusions may be drawn about the heavens; for the latter are too far away from us and too high in place and in rank.
>
> (*GP* II, 24; 326–7)

This passage does not have only limited interest for us; it is not just an example of out-dated physics. One puzzle which remains is exactly why Maimonides insists on the errors of the Ptolemaic system. After all, if he is right in demonstrating the incompatibility between Ptolemaic and Aristotelian principles, this could be taken to prove that different physical principles govern sublunar phenomena as compared with celestial events. This is in fact his argument to a degree, in that he suggests that Aristotelian physics must be limited to the sublunar world, but he also argues that whatever hypotheses apply to the heavens, they cannot be Ptolemaic. The reasoning seems at fault, since the latter system is criticized by virtue of its incompatibility with Aristotelianism, with which we should expect it to be incompatible given the different realms over which the different theories apply. Maimonides' point seems to be more secure than this objection suggests, though. He argues that Ptolemaic principles contravene not just Aristotelian physics, but any sort of physics which we could understand, and whatever physical principles apply to the heavens cannot be Ptolemaic.

Despite his disapproval of Ptolemaic physics, he is obliged to admit that it works in the sense of yielding accurate predictions of superlunar motion. According to Maimonides, whatever it is that produces these accurate predictions cannot be a theory in terms of either epicycles or eccentrics, but these may be used to good purpose as the results show. He makes the extraordinary claim that the astronomer is not concerned to represent the heavens as they really are, but is only interested in accurate predictions of motion. The mathematical models which astronomers use are perfectly adequate in so far as we are concerned with prediction, but they do not help us grasp the nature of the heavens. Maimonides suggests that one reason for this is that the heavens are really the province of divine rather than human knowledge, and as we have already seen, he criticizes the assumption that Aristotelian principles can be justifiably extended to cover both sublunar and celestial phenomena. What makes astronomical judgments concerning the heavens true is their accuracy, not the fact that anything corresponds to the way in which they picture the celestial phenomena.

On Maimonides' argument, it is a mistake to think of a conflict arising between these two competing theories. Both theories are valid if we bear in mind the limitations they embody. Aristotelian physics cannot offer an accurate model of the planets, nor can it provide a useful indication of their movements. It can explain the motion of bodies in the sublunar world since we know what principles govern those phenomena. We understand how such phenomena work:

> All that Aristotle states about that which is beneath the sphere of the moon is in accordance with reasoning: these are things that have a known cause, that follow one upon the other, and concerning which it is clear and manifest at what points wisdom and natural providence are effective.
>
> (*GP* II, 24; 326)

Ptolemaic physics produces accurate mathematical models of the superlunary world which at least helps us to grasp the fact that planetary movements are in accordance with some law, but what the laws actually are which apply to the planets only someone of superior intelligence to ourselves could appreciate.

What is the relevance of this discussion to Maimonides' more general points about creation and prophecy? One of the implications we can draw is that he should be taken seriously when he argues that we cannot discover the exact nature of the origin of the universe. The notion that if we can have no experience of an event then we can form no accurate judgment of it is far from ludicrous. On the contrary, the creation of the world (were such an event to have taken place) is even more remote from us than the present arrangement of the planets, and is completely inaccessible to us now in a way that the planets are not. We can at least observe the planets from our sublunary vantage point and make accurate calculations about them, while the putative starting point of the whole system is not available to us from any vantage point at all. Now, if we take Maimonides at face value in his discussion of astronomy, there appears to be no good reason to refuse to accept that he genuinely did not think that there is a demonstrative answer to the problem of the origination of the world. He clearly rejects the proofs for creation *ex nihilo* produced by the *kalām* (*GP* I, 71; 175–84). He clearly adheres to the value of Aristotelianism as an analytical model in understanding the structure of this world. But he argues quite convincingly that there is no reason to extend Aristotelianism to a level of reality of which we have no experience.

This has seemed like an evasion to most commentators, but there is much to be said for this argument. When we are considering the sorts of objects with which we are familiar we may find it impossible to abandon the basic Aristotelian principles relating to change, motion and matter. For instance, in the example of something suddenly coming into existence, or just as suddenly going out of existence, without relating to a persisting matter which Aristotle used to help explain the possibility of change would be problematic for our understanding of the everyday world. We could undoubtedly make the attempt at convincing ourselves of the possibility of such an event taking place, but it would be argued that a whole conceptual can of worms would thereby be opened. It would imply that part of our world was completely without explanation or rationale, and whatever might be said about this, there is no doubt that we would be involved in a very different conceptual scheme from the one we presently inhabit. After all, we may never discover the relationship between one event and another in our world, but it is basic to our understanding of that world that we presuppose that events are causally interrelated, and that the sorts of questions we ask of the world are sensible questions and appropriate to the phenomena which they address. No such difficulties arise, though, with looking at celestial events in a different way. For example, if one conceives of a planet suddenly coming in or going out of existence for no apparent reason, this does not throw our understanding of the everyday world into turmoil. Provided our everyday experience does not alter, there is no reason to rule out *a priori* the introduction of objects *ex nihilo* into the superlunary world. It would be assumed that those objects had an effect upon the sorts of events with which we are familiar, but the important aspect of this relationship is that we do not need to change our view of our commonsense world, nor our ability to make accurate predictions of the movement of the heavens. Why should it be assumed that the same physical principles and laws govern the celestial world as do our ordinary world? Why not take Maimonides at his word when he argues that:

> everything that Aristotle expounds with regard to the sphere of the moon and that which is above it is, except for certain things, something analogous to guessing and conjecturing. All the more does this apply to what he says about the order of the intellects and to some of the opinions regarding the divine which he believes; for the latter contain grave incongruities and perversities that manifestly and clearly appear as such to all the nations, that propagate evil, and that he cannot demonstrate.
>
> (*GP* II, 22; 319–20)

This is not a patently insincere comment. We know in Maimonides' view that Aristotelian physics is inappropriate to explain the motion of the planets, and we might wonder about the applicability of Aristotelian metaphysics to this realm of discourse. We know also, according to Maimonides, that miracles and the Law depend upon creation *ex nihilo*, and if we accept the line of argument he offers we might agree that demonstration is inapplicable when we talk about the nature of the origins of the world.

What depends upon the notion of creation *ex nihilo*? We have seen that miracles and the Law depend on it, but incorporeality, existence, and unity of the deity do not. The latter three attributes (although they should not be treated as attributes when applied to

76

the deity, of course) are equally derivable from whatever view one adopts on creation:

> As to this my method, it is as I shall describe to you in a general way now. Namely, I shall say: the world cannot but be either eternal or created in time. If it is created in time, it undoubtedly has a creator who created it in time . . . If, however, the world is eternal, it follows necessarily because of this and that proof that there is an existent other than all the bodies to be found in the world; an existent who is not a body and not a force in a body and who is one, permanent and sempiternal; who has no cause and whose becoming subject to change is impossible . . . Thus it has become manifest to you that the proofs for the existence and the oneness of the deity and His not being a body ought to be procured from the starting point afforded by the supposition of the eternity of the world, for in this way the demonstration will be perfect, both if the world is eternal and if it is created in time.
>
> (*GP* I, 71; 181–2)

The nature of the deity as incorporeal, unified and existing is not dependent upon any particular theory of the world's creation. It is thus logically preferable to seek to derive this conclusion from the most unsympathetic premises. The reason for the dependence of the Law and miracles upon a particular view of creation is not difficult to discover. With creation *ex nihilo* comes the idea of a purposive deity who can really choose between alternatives, and who intervenes in natural processes and establishes laws for his chosen community. But is it not surprising that such an important presupposition of the basis of religion should be a rather dubious proposition? While we may accept that belief in God, and an incorporeal, unified and living God at that, can be acquired by any theory of the world's origin, it is remarkable that the most basic principles of a particular religion rest on an apparently flimsy notion which is impossible to prove. Again, this is read by many commentators as Maimonides signalling to his more sophisticated audience that he does not really think there are adequate grounds for a justified belief in creation *ex nihilo*.

Before we accept this view and abandon the careful reasoning which Maimonides appears to present for the preferability of creation *ex nihilo*, it is worth returning to some of the basic aspects of his system. Firstly, like all the *falāsifa* he distinguished sharply between different groups of believers, and different kinds of language which are appropriate to them. It would be a mistake to address the ordinary members of the community as though they were philosophically skilled, and vice versa. The language we use must be sufficiently fluid to allow for a variety of meanings to be read into the same scriptural text with the result that different audiences gain enlightenment through their contact with the text. As one would expect, such a theory places great reliance upon the way in which language responds to such a challenge, and the language of the Bible is replete with equivocation which provides different readings for different readers. A good deal of the *Guide* is taken up with discovering and discussing equivocal terms, and there can be no doubt in the mind of any reader that the language which might immediately seem obvious in its intentions in the Biblical text is very far from being simple. It is worth emphasizing here that the idea is not that the more intellectually inclined receive the true message, while the ordinary people only obtain a pale reflection of the truth, or indeed nothing more than a pack of lies which nonetheless motivates them to behave in appropriate ways. Everyone receives the truth, but the truth is presented in such a way that it will enable them to make use of it in their decisions concerning how they are to behave, and what they are to believe.

This might seem itself to be an equivocation. After all, creation *ex nihilo* might be seen as the exoteric version of the esoteric doctrine of the eternity of the world. Maimonides might be taken to believe that really the world is eternal, and the philosophically sophisticated readers of his work will understand that this is his belief. Since the more simple readers and religious believers will find this belief difficult to reconcile with their notion of a purposive and powerful God, they are led to accept Maimonides' adherence to the notion of creation *ex nihilo*. This misinterpretation is caused by over-enthusiasm for the notion of equivocation. Maimonides argues that much language is equivocal, and as such can be used in a variety of distinct ways which are nonetheless linked, albeit tenuously. But it will be recalled that not just one notion of equivocation is used by Maimonides. When it comes to comparing human with divine attributes, there is no link between the names except for the names themselves. We need to be as sophisticated in our use of the two forms of equivocation as Maimonides is if we are to grasp his point here.

Let us look at the metaphysical consequences of the two types of equivocation. When a term is equivocal in the sense of being amphibolous there is a relationship between its uses in different contexts, but the relationship lies in an accidental rather than an essential feature which is common to both uses. This is appropriate when we are comparing two different points of view which are nonetheless both of the same species of creature. For example, both the philosopher and the ordinary believer talk about the will of God, and they interpret this differently. The former will perhaps try to understand this notion in terms of the actions of God as manifested in the world, while the latter will tend to think of God wanting to carry out actions in much the same way as we do, but on a larger scale. These two different uses are clearly linked, but very different. One use looks for the result of the will, while the other looks towards the mental process of willing which is presumed to have taken place. These uses are linked because the points of view from which they stem are linked. These points of view are both human points of view, and they express a range of understandings of a difficult yet important religious idea. Now, this form of equivocation is to be distinguished from that applicable to the use of terms to describe both human and divine attributes. Here we are not talking about differences which exist within a species, but very radical differences between totally unlike realms of discourse. There is an immense gulf between God and his creation, which Maimonides marks by his refusal to use the notion of *pros hen* equivocation. We can have no notion of what goes on in the divine realm, since we are inevitably limited by our characteristics of corruptibility and finitude. Hence we cannot know what attributes God possesses other than those which he possesses as a result of the notion of a deity. Hence we cannot know what rules the planets follow, nor how the world came about. Maimonides' position on this last issue is perfectly in tune with his general account of the distinction between human and divine knowledge.

Some of the implications of this approach should be clearer now. Along with the theory of equivocal terms goes a theory of objectivity which is more complex than one might imagine from examining the text of the *Guide*. We have already seen in the discussion of prophecy how biblical stories like the events at Sodom and Gomorrah can be taken in a non-literal sense without affecting their objectivity. One might also point to Maimonides' account of the equivocal nature of the term 'Adam' in the Bible. In *GP* I, 14 he argues that this term may be understood as the name of the first human being, the species of human being, or human beings as a collection of things. The references to 'Adam' may be taken in a literal and historical sense to describe what actually happened to a particular individual, or they may be taken in a figurative sense, to illustrate the nature of human beings, where their duty lies and what fate is in store for them if they go against the obligations laid on them by God. Now, in the *Guide* Maimonides uses 'Adam' in a variety of ways, sometimes as a historical subject and sometimes as an indication of broader issues. For example, when he comes to discuss Adam's sons in *GP* I, 7 he seems to take it for granted that it is a particular individual's biological children who are at issue. On the other hand, when he refers to them again in *GP* II, 30 he makes clear his view that they are part of a parable relating to the Garden of Eden, and the 'sons' are really an expression for Adam's thoughts. It could be that these thoughts are the thoughts produced by an individual person, or that they are taken to be products of a representative of the human species. They would fulfil their role in the story regardless of the exact nature of their provenance.

Why does this equivocation persist in the Bible? Why does the text not reveal clearly its intentions and state without obfuscation what the meaning of the text is? The reason is that the text has to satisfy a variety of different audiences, and these audiences are best addressed in a variety of different ways. Rather than have a number of different scriptures appropriate to those audiences, it is better to have just one text which can be interpreted differently. In this way the notion that basically there is just one message which is to be transmitted to the community can be preserved. All the different ways of interpreting a text have a purpose:

> Know that all the stories that you will find mentioned in the Torah occur there for a necessary utility of the Law; either they give a correct notion of an opinion that is a pillar of the Law, or they rectify some action so that mutual wrongdoing and aggression should not occur between men. I shall set this forth to you in a orderly fashion. As it is a pillar of the Law that the world was produced in time, that at first a single individual

of the human species, namely, Adam, was created, and that approximately two thousand five hundred years elapsed between Adam and Moses our Master, men, if they were given this information only, would rapidly have begun to have doubts in those times.

(*GP* III, 50; 613)

They would have doubts because they would fail to see the connection which links them and their various countries and languages with their original ancestors, so it is necessary to present an account which persuades people in general that they are linked to particular original events. This is Maimonides' explanation for the rather tedious enumeration of genealogies in the Bible. They are designed to help people think of themselves as part of a pattern and order in human development, and for this reason these stories and parables have a vital part to play in helping bring about adherence to the Law and an understanding of how it is to be followed.

Yet we return to the issue which has so far evaded a satisfactory solution. If belief in the creation of the world *ex nihilo* is so important (a pillar of the Law, we are told at *GP* III, 50), is it not surprising that it is a belief which cannot be demonstrated? After all, if we base our behaviour upon a belief which turns out to be false, or at the very least dubious, is this not a definition of recklessness? We should ensure that the presuppositions of our action are well-founded and based on truth before we use them to accomplish our purposes. This belief in creation *ex nihilo* seems to share the status of a good tip which someone might be given when entering a betting shop as to the merits of a particular horse in a race, and this is hardly the sort of grounding which one would want such an important religious notion to possess. The answer which Maimonides could produce to this objection is that the objectivity of the presupposition lies in the relationship between the presupposition and that which it makes possible. As long as we know that the proposition in the presupposition is possible we are justified in acting on it. What is important is how we behave, and if we base our behaviour upon a proposition which turns out to be false, and yet our behaviour is in accordance with appropriate rules of conduct, religious or otherwise, then that behaviour is perfectly well-founded.

This might appear to be a very dubious doctrine, and difficult to find in Maimonides' text. It will be argued here that this is his view, and an interesting and valuable analysis of a persistent problem in metaphysics. He compares our belief in the existence of God with our knowledge of his essence thus:

> We have mentioned in one of the chapters of this Treatise that there is an immense difference between guidance leading to a knowledge of the existence of a thing and an investigation of the true reality of the essence and substance of that thing. The reason is that guidance leading to the knowledge of the existence of a thing can be had even if that should be through the accidents of the thing or through its acts or through a relation – which may be very remote from the thing – existing between the latter and things other than itself.
>
> (*GP* I, 46; 97)

The precise nature of the origin of the world is something on which we can never have accurate knowledge, although we know that the world is dependent upon a creator even if we assume that it is eternal. This belief in the existence and incorporeality of a creator is not sufficient on Maimonides' account to ground a consequent adherence to the Law and belief in the miracles. What is required for that is belief in the creation of the world in time. But is this a belief only required of the ordinary people who appeal to figurative language when trying to make sense of what they are to do? Is it true that 'the belief is necessary for the abolition of reciprocal wrongdoing or for the acquisition of a noble moral quality – as, for instance, the belief that He . . . has a violent temper against those who do injustice' (*GP* III, 28; 514)?

We need to distinguish here between two types of figurative use of language. In one use we can observe language which is literally false, but with the intention of bringing about a beneficial result in its audience. This is the case with the illustration given above. If we follow Maimonides' attack on the anthropomorphic language surrounding the deity we can say that God is not ever in a temper or angry with people since this is an inappropriate way to describe the deity and his attributes. But although we know that God cannot be angry, we can still use this sort of language, which strictly is inaccurate, to get over a particular point. Now, the notion of the creation of the world in time is not like this sort of case. Here we are dealing with a proposition which, despite its significance, is not susceptible of demonstrative proof and yet can be shown to be possible. As Maimonides puts the point:

> For Alexander has explained that in every case in which no demonstration is possible, the two contrary opinions with regard to the matter in question should be posited as hypotheses, and it should be seen what doubts attach to each of them: the one to which fewer doubts attach should be believed. Alexander says that things are thus with respect to all the opinions regarding the divine that Aristotle sets forth and regarding which no demonstration is possible.
>
> (*GP* II, 22; 320)

And a little further on he produces his familiar assertion that:

> On the other hand, the belief in eternity the way Aristotle sees it – that is, the belief according to which the world exists in virtue of necessity, that no nature changes at all, and that the customary course of events cannot be modified with regard to anything – destroys the Law in its principle, necessarily gives the lie to every miracle, and reduces to inanity all the hopes and threats that the Law has held out.
>
> (*GP* II, 25; 328)

So it is absolutely vital in a religious sense that we act upon a proposition which we cannot prove to be true and against which there are solid, albeit not decisive, arguments.

Yet the question arises yet again of how we can base our religious beliefs upon such an apparently dubious proposition. Maimonides has two points to make in reply. The first is that it is a sign of intelligence that we appreciate where demonstration is possible and where it is not. Referring to Aristotle in the customary way, he says:

> When the chief of the philosophers began to investigate very obscure matters and to attempt a proof concerning them, he excused himself by making a statement the meaning of which was as follows. A student of his books should not, because of the subject of these researches, ascribe to him effrontery, temerity, and an excess of haste to speak of matters of which he had no knowledge; but rather he should ascribe to him the desire and

83

the endeavour to acquire and achieve true beliefs to the extent to which this is in the power of man

(*GP* I, 5; 29)

Calling for demonstration when it cannot be supplied is to fail to understand the difference which exists between different levels of discourse. The second point is to examine the notion of objectivity which Maimonides uses. When he was discussing the problems with Ptolemaic physics he argued that we could use it profitably even though we know that it cannot offer an accurate description of how the planets interact. What matters are the results which we can derive from the mathematical model presented by that hypothesis. A similar line may be taken with some of the biblical parables. They can be taken to be historical accounts, but their real import is to illustrate how we are to behave in ways which are accessible to the largest possible audience in the community. Whether the history they describe occurred or not does not matter; these accounts are perfectly objective if they help us appreciate where our duty lies. This is the approach which Maimonides would take with respect to creation *ex nihilo*. This can be taken to be an historical event, but it is not important if it turns out that the world was not produced in that way. If we only believe in it then we can adhere to the requirements of religion, and especially the Law.

5

The assault on the *kalām*

Maimonides spends a good deal of the *Guide* attacking the *kalām* and it is worth considering carefully why he thinks this such an important task. His approach is not immediately very different from the rest of the *falāsifa*, and there are marked similarities between his critique and that of Averroes (*A*, pp. 144–60). Theology is all well and good if restricted to a particular sphere, which is helping the community of believers understand difficulties in the interpretation of religious texts. Rules have grown up based upon commentaries and the teaching of generations of scholars and pious individuals, and within the context of a particular religion it is important to have a set of ideas and traditions which helps the community at large resolve difficulties which are bound to arise in the formulation of religious law and doctrine to match the changing conditions under which the community finds itself. Maimonides is himself an outstanding theologian whose influence upon Jewish law and theology has remained powerful to this day. What is it about theology, then, that aroused the suspicion and ire of so many *falāsifa* during the Middle Ages?

The problem with theology is that its adherents sometimes overstep the mark in questions of its applicability. Theology can operate quite successfully within a realm of discourse, but is entirely empty when considered from without that way of speaking. It has no power to persuade either intellectually or emotionally those people who do not share the religious beliefs of its community. Theological and religious arguments function by presupposing the rules of a particular religion or community as valid, and then exploring their implications for certain situations. It is helpful in this context to look at a passage from one of the main influences on Maimonides, Farabi, who suggests in his *Book of Letters* (p. 131) that:

> Since it was natural that demonstration be perceived after these [that is, dialectical and sophistical powers], it followed necessarily that dialectical and sophistical powers, as well as thinking, should have preceded in time certain philosophy, that is, demonstrative philosophy. And religion, considered as a human matter, is later in time than philosophy in general, since it is aimed at teaching the multitude theoretical and practical things which were deduced in philosophy through ways which facilitate the multitude's understanding of them, either through persuasion, or representation, or through both of them together. The arts of theology and jurisprudence are later in time than religion and are subordinate to it. And if the religion is subordinate to an ancient philosophy, either based on opinion, or on sophistical thinking, then the theology and the jurisprudence which are subordinate to it accord with either of them but are below either of them.
>
> (Berman, 'Maimonides, the disciple of Alfarabi', pp. 157–8; I would prefer the translation 'imagination' to replace 'representation' above).

According to Farabi, dialectical and sophistical modes of thinking preceded demonstrative philosophy, which was itself followed by religion.

> Religion consists of opinions and actions, determined and limited by conditions, which their first ruler lays down to the group, seeking to achieve a specific goal which he has, either in them or by means of them, through their active utilization of these opinions and actions.
>
> (Berman, 'Maimonides, the disciple of Alfarabi', p. 159)

The relationship between philosophy and religion is an interesting one. The leader of the community is taken to be a philosopher and capable of establishing a religion which is in tune with the thinking and customs of his particular time and place. He combines the intellectual ability to think demonstratively about matters of ultimate significance with the political skill to relate those issues to ordinary people in ways which are meaningful to them.

What one has to bear in mind in this approach to the relationship of philosophy and theology is that the former is taken to embody the most perfect and abstract of reasoning processes, while the latter merely defends the principles of religion set out in a particular community's sacred and legal texts. This division of labour is not necessarily intended to be disparaging towards theology, but is rather an attempt at putting it in its logical place. It necessarily deals with far more restricted material than does philosophy, and it assumes that the principles of a particular religion are valid. Philosophy is itself capable of assessing such principles, accepting some and rejecting others, but the theologian must take for granted his premisses and see what they imply. It is important to separate theology from philosophy since people might regard the rather poor arguments often produced by the former as representative of the best philosophy can do in the support of certain doctrines. This leads to opposition to philosophy and to a decline in belief in the doctrines themselves which theology tries to prove, and both these effects were regarded as damaging by the *falāsifa*.

Maimonides falls into line with this general philosophical strategy in the *Guide*. He ends the first part with his account of the history of the *kalām* which developed first in Christianity, then moved to Islam and Judaism. The point of the *kalām* is to defend religion against the claims of the philosophers which appear to contradict quite basic religious doctrines, and so the theologians (*mutakallimūn*) 'started to establish premisses that would be useful to them with regard to their belief and to refute those opinions that ruined the foundations of their Law' (*GP* I, 71; 177). One of the tasks which the theologians set themselves in particular was the proof that the world is created in time, from which they sought to derive the conclusion that it has a maker who created it in time and who is unified and incorporeal (*GP* I, 71; 179). Maimonides criticizes their approach since 'every argument deemed to be a demonstration of the temporal creation of the world is accompanied by doubts and is not a cogent demonstration except among those who do not know the difference between demonstration, dialectics, and sophistic argument' (*GP* I, 71; 180). Anyone who understands these issues has to acknowledge, according to Maimonides, that there is no decisive answer to the problem of the origin of the world and to base the proof for the existence of an incorporeal and unified deity on such a flimsy foundation is to court disaster. Maimonides argues that a far more successful way of establishing the existence of such a deity is to assume that the world is eternal, from which a valid proof can be constructed to the appropriate conclusion. In that case it does not matter precisely how the world has come about, since even the hardest possible premises we can use to get the conclusion we want will serve that purpose.

The only valid way to establish the existence of God is to start by rejecting the premises of the theologians. In *GP* I, 73 he sets out twelve premises which are basic to the theological attempts to demonstrate that the world has a beginning in time and that God exists in a unified and incorporeal state. In Chapter 74 he produces seven arguments which they use to establish the creation of the world in time, in Chapter 75 he discusses five proofs of the unity of God, and in the next chapter there are three attempts at showing that God is incorporeal. His verdict on all these efforts by the theologians is that:

> they have abolished the nature of being and have altered the original disposition of the heavens and the earth by thinking that by means of those premises, it would be demonstrated that the world was created in time. As a result they have not demonstrated the creation of the world in time and have destroyed for us the demonstrations of the existence and oneness of the deity and of the negation of his corporeality. For the demonstrations, by means of which all this can be made clear, can only be taken from the permanent nature of what exists, a nature that can be seen and apprehended by the sense and the intellect.
>
> (*GP* I, 76; 230–1).

He follows up the rather destructive approach of these chapters with Part Two of the *Guide* which seeks to show how the operation of proving the existence, unity, and incorporeality of God should be carried out. He produces twenty-five premises which he argues are demonstrable, and a twenty-sixth, stating that time and motion are eternal, which he will accept as an hypothesis but not as demonstrable. He tries to take up a position on this premiss which mediates between Aristotle's commentators who think this premiss is necessary and true, and the theologians who try to disprove it entirely.

The way in which Maimonides sets about establishing the existence of God and his basic characteristics is interesting. The theologians proceed first of all by arguing that the whole nature of reality is dependent upon God for its nature and existence, and that everything which takes place in the world is only capable of so behaving because of divine fiat. God makes decisions about the way in which the world is to operate, and these are entirely a result of his freely functioning will. The sort of model which the Ash'arite theologians in particular had in mind was one of atoms which are themselves insubstantial and only existent for a minute period of time, so that there is the necessity for a deity to hold everything together and produce the sort of world of which we have experience. Really, there are no material objects in existence, just atoms going in and out of existence very rapidly, and the decisions we take about what we are doing are merely reflections of what God permits us to do by his willing certain actions on our part to take place. It obviously follows that what we think of as natural laws and regularities are only apparently so, since they represent the ways in which God has chosen to act over a particular period, and there is no justification for thinking that they will remain the same and give us good grounds for future predictions. Everything which exists is a function of divine will, and they only have the solidity and regularity which they have because of this supernatural connection. They could be dissolved at any time God wishes, and new things brought into existence. The world is radically contingent and dependent upon its creator. God can bring into existence anything (logically possible) that he wishes and can destroy it with equal ease, and he need not have created in the way in which he has. If we are to understand what it is that really exists, we must look behind the veil of the material world to the will which makes everything and controls everything which appears to exist independently (*A*, pp. 52–63).

Maimonides also argued that the world is dependent upon God, but in a very different way than that presented by Ghazali and the Ash'arite theologians. He followed a basically Aristotelian analysis in which there are four types of cause which explain the nature and behaviour of material objects. He also adhered to the view of Avicenna on the distinction between essence and existence (in marked contrast to Averroes: *A*, pp. 104–16). This distinction regards existence as a property which things have when they exist, and a property which they acquire when they are brought into existence by some cause which necessitates that existence. It gives rise to the further distinction between God, who is necessarily existent through himself and without any external cause for existence, and everything else, which is possible in itself and necessitated by something else. Averroes accused this theory of merely replacing the occasionalism of Ghazali with another type of occasionalism based this time not on the will of God but on the effect of a determining cause (*A*, pp. 115–16). Material objects themselves thus appear to have no properties in themselves, but only as recipients of existence from a necessitating cause. In any case, Maimonides uses the distinction devised by Avicenna to organize a proof for the existence of God which argues from the status of the world as something possible in itself to the need for a cause which is the only existent necessary in itself (*GP* II, 1; 247–9).

What it is important to grasp about Maimonides' account of the natural world is its status in his model of how to do philosophy. The theologians argue that the natural world is merely a collection of epiphenomena of the undetermined will of God. What we think of as the necessary link between cause and effect is just the result of our becoming accustomed to the way in which God's will works, together with the effect on our minds of ideas placed there directly by the deity (with the intention of helping us make sense of the natural world). The approach which the theologians use to threaten the necessity of the causal nexus is the thought-experiment. Can we not imagine, they say, a cause occurring without its effect following on from it, and vice versa? It is not easy to think about such alterations to our everyday experience, yet surely not impossible. The reader of this page believes that the world behind him, with which he is not presently in visual contact, has a certain form, so that were he to turn around he would see much the same scene as he saw before his eyes moved to the book. Yet it is not impossible to imagine that one has been transported by some supernatural force to the Arctic wastes, or the jungles of South America, while reading this page, and when one turns around one is amazed at what has happened. One might classify such experience as a dream, yet this need not necessarily be the only interpretation. It is not logically inconceivable for very radical transformations to occur to what we take for granted about our world, and the theologians argue that this shows that we should be wary in claiming any necessity in a particular interpretation of how the world works. The world could quite suddenly come to work in different ways without any logical laws being broken, and we should then become aware of how dogmatic our belief in the necessity of the cause-effect relation is. It is not necessary to establish this point that this extraordinary change in our experience actually takes place. All that is necessary is that we should be able to contemplate such a change, and if our imagination can stretch that distance it shows that there is no necessity in our causal laws other than their familiarity and our unwillingness to challenge them.

This argument is cleverly developed by Ghazali in his *Refutation of the Philosophers* (*A*, pp. 52–63: *I*, pp. 74–86), and it is clearly the formulation which Maimonides has in mind when he comes to criticize the theologians. The presupposition of their approach upon which he concentrates is their principle that 'everything that may be imagined is an acceptable notion for the intellect' (*GP* I, 73; 206 – I prefer the translation 'acceptable' here for Pines' 'admissible' as more appropriate for *tajwīz*). The principle suggests that anything which we can represent to ourselves as a possible state of affairs is thereby proved to be conceivable, and a real challenge to the counter-claim that there are necessary aspects of our everyday experience of the world. Maimonides does go on to weaken his formulation of the theologians' principle by accepting that they do accept that there are necessary relationships between particular concepts, and again he probably had Ghazali in mind here, but it leaves us with the general point that the imagination is a powerful conceptual tool in the elucidation of the distinction between strict logical necessity from the putative necessity which appears to link aspects of the natural world. According to Maimonides, it is appropriate to use the intellect to establish relationships which are genuinely necessary; the imagination is incapable of performing this function, and the ways in which Ghazali tries to extend its use to cover a large variety of different natural events is not valid. When we try to establish relationships of necessity between concepts we are trying to link universal and abstract notions, and the universal is a product of the sort of abstraction which is the province of the intellect. The imagination, on the other hand, is far more closely aligned to the faculty of sensation, and there is no inherent limit on the ways in which it can combine and assemble images. There is no requirement for questions of truth and falsity to arise when we consider such images, they just exist in a particular way, whereas the contents of our intellectual efforts are subject to considerations of truth value. The imagination is a confused ragbag of representations of what is not the case and what cannot be the case. It is limited, moreover, in that it cannot always represent what we have good rational grounds for believing to be true.

Now, these remarks about the limitations of the imagination are quite reasonable, and represent a different approach to philosophical reasoning from that followed by Ghazali and the *kalām*. They use thought-experiments to show that statements which the Aristotelians hold as necessary are imaginable as not existing in the way specified by the rules. They conclude that this shows such 'necessary' claims are not necessary at all. Maimonides suggests that a mere exercise of imagination is not sufficient to destroy the necessity of a claim, since 'It is by means of the intellect that the universal is differentiated from the individual, and no demonstration is true except by means of universals. It is also through the intellect that essential predicates are discerned from accidental ones' (*GP* I, 73; 207). When we make truth claims about anything we are using abstract and universal concepts which specify the type of object we are describing, and relating it to a particular example. When we come to distinguish between those properties which a thing has which are essential to its being that sort of thing and other properties which it might have or might not, we are clearly using abstract notions of what it is for such a thing to satisfy the criteria appropriate to it. The implication which Maimonides wants to draw here is that the thought-experiments of the theologians may well succeed in producing an apparent counter-example to a necessity established by philosophy, but this might be brought about by sleight of hand, in that only the accidental as opposed to the essential aspects of the things involved might be altered by the imagination. The result of such an exercise would not, then, be capable of attacking the philosophical claim that a particular relationship of necessity obtains between the essential properties of the thing. For example, we can imagine with Ghazali a piece of cotton brought into contact with fire and not burning. But this does not show by itself that it is conceivable for such an event to take place.

Maimonides acknowledges that the *kalām* does not present a crude account of possibility which is easy to knock down. For example, the theologians do not argue that anything we can imagine is thereby shown to be possible. Maimonides gives the examples of two contrary properties coming together in the same place and time, an atom existing without any properties, the change of a thing into an accident and the reverse, and the penetration of one atom by another (*GP* I, 73; 207). Ghazali would accept these imaginable states of affair as nonetheless impossible because of what is meant by the terms in such claims. We might try to imagine them and think we had succeeded, but this could only be accomplished through doing violence to what is meant by the terms in the claims. What Maimonides finds basically unsatisfactory about the atomism of the theologians is that it does not explain anything. Everything is taken to be at the beck and call of something which is not itself in the world, and the pattern of change and alteration which we appear to observe in the world is nothing more than a misleading appearance behind which the real causal factors operate. The view of the world which the *kalām* presents is rather like a play in which the *deus ex machina* operates at every stage to make things happen, and it is not difficult to imagine how unsatisfactory such a play would be from a dramatic point of view. If we can perfectly well observe how the world works as an inter-connected unit with necessary laws of nature and regular behaviour manifesting itself at every turn, why look for a supernatural level of explanation which would overturn all this organization? Maimonides is not just arguing in a dogmatic way that because the world has a particular form it must always have had that form, or that that structure is necessary. This would contravene his Principle. He goes further than this, as does the creator of the model he so enthusiastically uses. Aristotle's point was not that because the world has a certain form, it must have that form. The argument is stronger than this. It proceeds from the phenomena with which we are familiar to argue that it follows from what we mean when we talk about objects and their properties that there are substances, they change in particular ways, and there is a necessary pattern to their behaviour. This is a fact about our view of the world and it enters into what we mean when we talk about things and the place which we and they have in a common world.

It is important for Maimonides to be able to distinguish between the way in which things are and the way in which they might be for his central claim about the possibility of creation *ex nihilo*. As he puts it:

For if the philosopher says, as he does: That which exists is my witness and by means of it we discern the necessary, the possible and the impossible, the adherent of the Law says to him: The dispute between us is with regard to this point. For we claim that that which exists was made in virtue of will and was not a necessary consequence. Now if it was made in this fashion, it is admissible that it should be made in a different way, unless intellectual representation decides, as you think it decides, that something different from what exists at present is not admissible . . . about that I have something to say, which you will learn in various passages of this Treatise. It is not something one hastens to reject in its entirety with nonchalance.

(*GP* I, 73; 211)

The reply which 'the adherent of the Law' makes to the Aristotelian is that it is possible to conceive intellectually of a state of affairs which might be called the creation of the world out of nothing. This is possible, Maimonides argues, because even if we grant everything the Aristotelian asserts are constant and essential features of the world, we are nonetheless justified in wondering whether there was a state of affairs describable as that existing before the creation of the world. Certainly, we can say that 'after motion has come into existence . . . one cannot imagine that it should come into being as a whole and perish as a whole' (*GP* II, 17; 297), but this failure to imagine such a state of affairs does not mean that it could not exist. It is rather like the failure of the imagination to represent perfectly valid possibilities. He gives the example of a hyperbola whose assymptotes come closer and closer to the curve. According to the imagination the lines approaching one another must ultimately meet, and so the hyperbola and its assymptotes must finally intersect. But we can prove that the two can never intersect (*GP* I, 73; 210). He wants to be limited neither to the narrowness of the imagination nor to the nature of the world as it presently is in his articulation of the notion of possibility.

This attempt at mediating between these contrary doctrines places him on something of a conceptual tightrope. One reason why it is important for him to distinguish the type of causality appropriate to sublunar as opposed to celestial agents is the necessity to stress the essential difference between those two forms of agency. When it is a question of the sort of efficient causality in the natural world:

It has been made clear in the natural sciences that every body that acts in some manner upon another body does this only

through encountering it or through encountering something that
encounters it, if this agent acts through an intermediary . . . [by
contrast] the action of the separate intellect is always designated
as an overflow, being likened to a source of water that overflows
in all directions and does not have one particular direction from
which it draws while giving its bounty to others.

(*GP* II, 12; 277)

The process of emanation through which the incorporeal intellects
affect the spatio-temporal world takes as lawlike and regular a form
as does the efficient causality with which we are familiar. We can
use the picture of emanation to work back from the effect to the
nature of the cause, and this gives rise to the intriguing possibility
that we might be able to discover aspects of the divine nature from
the evidence of its effects. Maimonides does, after all, suggest that
' "overflow" is sometimes applied in Hebrew to God, may he be
exalted, with the view of likening him to an overflowing spring of
water . . . for nothing is more fitting as a simile of action of one
that is separate from matter than this expression . . . "overflow" '
(*GP* II, 12; 279). He also claims that 'God . . . is the efficient cause
of the world, its form and end' (*GP* I, 69; 167). It might be thought
that we are receiving here useful information about the way in
which God brought the world into being, but in reality we are
receiving nothing of the kind. Through his constant activity God
affects both the material bodies of the world and the incorporeal
intellects, but how he does it is beyond our awareness. All we can
know is what it is that God brings about, not how and why he
creates in a particular way.

When he talks about the origin of the world, Maimonides is
careful to avoid descriptions which involve either causality as we
experience it in the material world or emanation as it is supposed
to relate the incorporeal bodies and the material world. As for the
former, he is firm that 'God's bringing the world into existence does
not have a temporal beginning, for time is one of the created things'
(*GP* II, 13; 282). Since the notion of time presupposes the existence
of motion, there is no point in talking about the time which existed
before the world was set in motion. He dismisses the emanation
model for reasons which he might well have found in Ghazali, that
since from something simple and unified only something else simple
and unified could proceed, this is no likely explanation for the

production of the many and various items in the material world by a single creator (*GP* II, 22). Whatever it is that we can say about the way in which the world was created – and we are very limited in the detail we can enter into here – it is inappropriate to claim that it came about through a process which was necessary in the way that the events of our world come about. The theologians go to the other extreme and see the divine will and a complete absence of necessity everywhere. Maimonides is working towards a conclusion which shows that God 'wills only what is possible, and not everything that is possible, but only that which is required by his wisdom to be in that state' (*GP* III, 25; 505). God is powerful and free enough to bring about a world with maximum disorder and suffering for living creatures, but being the sort of agent he is, he decided to bring about our sort of world which manifests in its structure the wisdom and goodness of its creator.

Let us examine the strength of Maimonides' general argument here. He presents a host of arguments which are designed to support his case, and a large number of criticisms of the approach of the theologians, and occasionally of Aristotle and his commentators. These can be found in the text of the *Guide* and will not be discussed directly here. His approach to the *kalām* is to argue that they misinterpret the data which confront them when they observe the events of the world. They refuse to allow the existence of necessary connections and posit a hidden supernatural force which lies behind natural phenomena. They suggest that we can perfectly easily contemplate a world in which there are exceptions to such putative necessary connections and that we require an account of nature which pays due respect to the power and influence of an individual and wise deity. Maimonides' distinction between imagination and intellect is very interesting here. He suggests that an apparently successful exercise of the imagination may not yield a proposition which is capable of receiving a truth value. The fact that we can manage to imagine a supernatural explanation behind every physical connection does not show that such a claim is a contribution to our understanding of the nature of such connection. We can imagine all sorts of things invisibly affecting what we see, and yet it is only sensible to talk about such causal agents if they can be argued to make some difference to the nature of our experience. Would God really concern himself with every specific detail of the material world? What is added to our understanding of the nature of the physical world by the hypothesis that every event in it is directly brought about by the deity? This is the strategy of opposition to the *kalām* which Maimonides adopts, and it is a very effective one.

So there are a number of bases to Maimonides' critique of the *kalām*. One is the unreliability of imagination and the lack of depth in explanations which involve imagination. To give an example which Maimonides uses, imagine a small child who lived entirely without female company on an island with only his father. When the child asks his father how he came about, the father might go into the mechanics of human reproduction. This might appear quite incredible to the child, since he might fail to understand how something can live within the body of another thing without suffocating (*GP* II, 17; 295–6). The imagination is clearly limited in the information which it can provide, and it must be distinguished from the entirely rational intellect. The theological argument schema is based upon the idea that there are particular premisses which are accepted for religious reasons, and which are then defended against possible objections. This is an inappropriate way of carrying out a philosophical reasoning, though, since this sort of reasoning has to work from necessary and already established premisses to the conclusions which are themselves also necessary and indubitable. According to Maimonides, the theological arguments not only fail to prove the conclusions which they seek to establish, but they throw into doubt those conclusions themselves, even though there are philosophically respectable ways of justifying them. A good example here is the treatment of the notion of creation *ex nihilo*. Maimonides argues that this notion is possible, and that there are good grounds for thinking it is true. The *kalām* argues that it is the only possible hypothesis available in the explanation of the origination of the world, and its arguments are so weak that they throw doubt upon the possibility of the notion and its connections with the characteristics of the deity.

Maimonides' critique of the Aristotelians takes a similar form to his approach to the *kalām*. The philosophers treat a principle – the eternity of the world – in their system as though it were something that could be demonstrated. They err in this, since there is no way that we can draw conclusions about the origin of the world from evidence of the nature of the world once it has been created. There are no good demonstrative arguments for the eternity of the world, and the philosophers, like the theologians, try to buttress up this important axiom in their system by arguments which are weak and are designed to establish the inconceivability of the contrary view. If we accept what we have called Maimonides' Principle here then we shall have to accept that there is no way of coming to any definite conclusion concerning the origin of the world. This might seem, and has seemed to generations of commentators, like something of an evasion. Did he really think that there was no successful and decisive argument which could settle this issue, especially given his open adherence to a great deal of the Aristotelian system?

There is very little to be gained by examining the psychology of Maimonides on this point. Let us just look at his argument. Maimonides' Principle suggests that there is a basic difference between the rules which exist within a system and the rules of the system itself. As such, it is an interesting and plausible thesis. For example, there are laws of nature, but it does not follow that the way in which nature itself is created follows such laws. There are rules in a game, but they do not themselves constitute the reason for the game. There is a difference between justifying a practice and justifying an action which falls within it. For example, the practice of keeping one's promises has a certain point which might not be shared by a particular instance in which the question as to whether one should keep one's promises arises. The point of the promising practice might be to benefit the widest possible group of citizens in a community, while in a particular case the only people concerned with an instance of breaking a promise might be positively disbenefited as a consequence.

This justification of Maimonides' Principle might seem rather lame. After all, he is very enthusiastic in his writings about paying due attention to the way in which things are organized in the world, and the decision to stop looking at the world in a causal way when we get above the moon seems rather arbitrary. Why should the same processes which we observe around us not govern the universe, and lead us to believe in an eternal universe? Maimonides is not being dogmatic here, but on the contrary he is appealing to evidence of disorder in the universe (leading to the notion of a creator) and to the distinction between the way the world is and how it came to be like that. This is enough to ground the possibility of the notion of creation out of nothing, and allows him to use this as a presupposition for much of the Jewish religion. Given the importance of this presupposition, though, it might be thought to be a problem that it cannot be demonstrated, but must merely be accepted as possible. This is not a problem for Maimonides. Those who have a sophisticated view of religion realize that all that we can really know about God is that he exists, is one and incorporeal. We can derive all this from the proposition that the world is eternal. Most people require religious language which is a good deal fuller than this, and so the notion of a created world becomes important. They can have that notion because there is nothing impossible about it.

6

What can God know?

The question of God's knowledge might seem an easy one to answer within the context of the notion of God employed by the Christians, Jews and Muslims. God is taken to know everything about everything, from the smallest and apparently unimportant detail to the most complex and abstract natural law. God is taken to have brought the world into being, and as its creator knows its every aspect. On the ordinary notion of reward and punishment in the next life, our ultimate fate is determined by God's awareness of our every action and decision on the basis of which he can make a fair judgment. In any case, the idea that once God has brought the world into being he turns his back on it and is unconcerned with what goes on in it is not acceptable from a religious point of view. On the other hand, there are great problems in making sense of the idea of knowing what goes on in the world when the subject is taken to be God. How can he be aware of ordinary events if he is without sensory equipment? Temporal and spatial phenomena change, are instantiated at one time and in one place and then change. If he is taken to be aware of all these events, his state of mind must be continually changing, as is the case with human beings, and yet God is supposed to be unchanging and unaffected by what goes on in the world. He cannot be said to find things out in the way in which we do, since we are affected by reality and form ideas about it, while God is in some way responsible for that reality and it can be no surprise to him that things turn out in one way rather than another way. Yet there are great problems in understanding how he could be aware of all the transient particulars which make up our world as particulars, how he could know that today I have toothache and yesterday I felt fine, how he could know that it snowed this morning and what I had for breakfast. Do we really expect God to know about these sorts of events?

This topic became controversial in Islamic philosophy since Avicenna produced his powerful argument for God's knowledge being limited to universals and unique events. Avicenna gets to this conclusion by exploring the notion of the appropriate objects for an omniscient being to know. These cannot be the transient and every-day events of our world, since these are always changing, and an immutable God cannot possess different mental attitudes depending upon the time he is observing the world. What God can know are the very general logical rules and necessary relationships which exist between abstract concepts, and this fits in well with the idea of God knowing his own essence which is that of thought thinking itself (*Metaphysics*, 1072b 18). In any case, it is more fitting to regard God as only knowing certain sorts of things and being concerned with the most pure and abstract relations as opposed to the hum-drum activities of our world of generation and corruption. This has the difficult consequence, though, that God then seems to become ignorant of great amounts of potential knowledge which is particular and yet important. For example, most of the Bible deals with par-ticular events and their consequences, and it can hardly be accept-able to assert that God does not know that Moses left Egypt or that Abraham made a covenant with him. It was precisely this point that led Ghazali to emphasize the importance of the notion of God knowing what goes on in the ordinary world in any meaningful notion of the deity (*I*, pp. 108–20). He argued in his *Tahāfut al-falāsifa* (Incoherence of the philosophers) and in the *Munqidh min al-ḍalāl* (Deliverer from error) that what the philosophers were really trying to do with their sophisticated notion of a God who only apprehends universals was to separate God from the world in such a way as to make his existence nugatory. If God is just an entity who contemplates very abstract concepts then the notion of a personal and concerned deity which is so important for a normal understanding of the Jewish and Muslim religions becomes inap-propriate.

Maimonides has a simple retort to this sort of objection in his theory of pure equivocation. All he has to do is argue that we get into this kind of confusion because we are mixing up two entirely different uses of the term 'knowledge'. There is human knowledge and there is divine knowledge, and they have nothing in common except the use of the same name (*GP* I, 56). If he had accepted a limited equivocation view like that of Averroes he could have argued that our notion of knowledge is a derivative of its most perfect and complete sense when used to describe God's knowledge. But the assertion that there is no problem in the notion of divine knowledge because we have no idea what that sort of knowledge actually is seems rather lame. And Maimonides does not leave it at that. He provides some detail on a possible answer to the issue. He is guarded in his comments upon Avicenna's thesis, claiming that 'knowledge has for its object the species, but in a certain way, applies to all the individuals of the species' (*GP* III, 20; 481). For Maimonides, a species has no independent existence apart from its individual constituents, and he accepts quite plainly that God knows 'with one knowledge the many and numerous things' (*GP* III, 20; 480). In the same place he asserts that God's knowledge extends to the infinite, to what possible things there are, and yet that it is unified and unchanging. God is unaffected by what he knows, and remains unified even though his objects of apprehension make up a plurality, and he remains unchanged despite their changing properties. To try to explain how this is possible he takes the example of the artisan contemplating his product and contrasts it with the knowledge that someone else has of it. God's knowledge of the objects he had brought about is not acquired through studying those objects, but rather it is the other way around. Those objects can be known in the way in which they can be known because of the ways in which God brought them about.

How does this example of the artisan at *GP* III, 21 advance our understanding of Maimonides' point? In the example he gives of someone who designs and builds a clock with a potentially infinite number of movements he contrasts the knowledge of its maker with that of its observer. One interesting aspect of the contrast is that the observer has to try to understand what will happen to the clock in the future, where this might involve an infinite variety and number of movements. The implication is that the artisan can comprehend these features of his product, but the observer cannot. Why does the artisan not have to inspect an infinity of movement before he can understand what the clock can do? The answer is straightforward. The creator understands the principle on which his product is based, and he does not require experience of its

operations to work out how it operates. For Maimonides the important aspect of a thing is its form, what makes it the thing it is and
defines it. The form of the clock which the artisan has in his mind
is what the clock is all about, and its eventual instantiation merely
makes concrete that idea and those principles of design. Knowing
the clock as a clock is a matter of understanding its form; knowing
the clock as a particular clock involves the actual thing which is
produced, the combination of form and matter. Does it not follow,
then, that what God knows are the formal principles which govern
the organization of material objects (and much else) but not the
objects themselves? This is not what Maimonides actually says. He
claims that God knows everything, and nothing is hidden from him
(*GP* III, 21). He is aware of everything, and his knowledge is
equivalent to his essence. He is even aware of the infinite. The
question really is how God knows rather than what he knows. He
knows in the way that a creator knows, by understanding the
principles upon which what exists is founded. We do not know
what will happen in the future, and we cannot know an infinite
number of changes, but the artisan knows what *form* future actions
of his creation will take. He does not have to wait to see what is
going to happen, because he knows. But saying that he knows what
is going to happen does not mean that he will be able to experience
all the events of watching the clock *ad infinitum*. This is by no means
necessary for any claim to know how the clock works to succeed.
The model which Maimonides appears to have in mind is that of
God being aware of the principles according to which things work,
while we have to work out the principles by a lengthy and necessarily incomplete observation of some of their actions.

One might think given Maimonides' general thesis of the complete lack of relationship between our knowledge and God's knowledge that he would warn his readers against trying to identify these
two activities. In *GP* III, 20 he is quite determined to warn people
off this sort of identification. Yet interestingly he argues at *GP* I,
68 that knowledge for human beings and for God is not merely
similar but actually the same. The argument is an interesting one.
Firstly, human beings are said to be potentially intelligent, by
contrast with other animals, where this means capable of using the
intellect. We receive information about the world through our sense
organs, and this information consists of both an image and a concept
by which the image can be recognized and categorized as an image

of something. When I see a clock I not only receive particular sensations of the visual kind but I am also able to classify what I see as a clock. If I am able to see a clock then I must be able to appreciate its clock-ness, i.e. what there is about it which makes it a clock. This sort of formal and abstract knowledge tells us precisely what it is that we have before us. Once we abstract from the actual clock to consider its form our thought of the form is identical with the form itself, and the person apprehending the form is identical with the form too.

What can we make of this claim? Not only is it puzzling, but it is supposed to apply not just to God but to us as well. This is hardly a normal Maimonidean claim. He claims that:

> Accordingly he is always the intellect as well as the intellectually cognizing subject and the intellectually cognized object. It is accordingly also clear that the numerical unity of the intellect, the intellectually cognizing subject, and the intellectually cognized object, does not hold good with reference to the creator only, but also with reference to every intellect . . . We, however, pass intellectually from potentiality to actuality only from time to time.
> (*GP* I, 68; 165–6).

On the Aristotelian account of intellectual knowledge which Maimonides is using here the intellect is seen as rather like the sensory faculties. It waits to be affected by something coming from outside of it: in the case of the mind, essences. The mind is potentially the same as its object in the sense that it has no actual existence until it receives something. All we can say about the mind is that it has the capacity to receive, and once it has received it is equivalent to what it has received. The analogy between the mind and the sensory faculties is not, of course, complete. The latter requires physical faculties unlike the mind (*De Anima*, 429a 7) and the mind only perceives essences of things, that which defines them. This seems hard to accept. Why should we compare sensing something (my toes sense the cold by becoming cold when placed on ice) and thinking something (my mind thinks of ice by becoming an image of the essence of ice)? We get this sort of language because of the importance for Aristotle of the imagination as a necessary condition of our thinking processes. When one looks into the mind, were that to be possible, one would see a collection of images of essences, and that is all. The mind is identical with what is in it since Aristotle regards it as nothing more than a capacity to have such content. Were we to be asked to make a list of things which existed we could include the contents of the mind but not the mind itself as something separate from that content.

This is how he arrives at the thesis that when the mind is apprehending something it is identical to that thing. In our case we have to wait to be affected by thoughts which arrive from outside of us in the sense that the active intellect sets our material intellect in motion. There is nothing causal going on here, but rather it is a matter of our intellectual thought being dependent upon acquiring formal concepts which may take some time to achieve, and which will never be fully acquired, given the imperfections in human knowledge. For God, by contrast, the store of formal concepts are all there as part of his essence, and he is perpetually thinking about them and using them. They express his essence. For God, then, it is easy to see why there is identity not only between the object of thought and the mind which has the thought but also between both these aspects of his essence and God as a subject. God is regarded on the Aristotelian principle as thought thinking itself, and he is nothing other than the contents of his thinking processes. This is not to posit a restriction in divine knowledge, since those thinking processes contain the most perfect formal knowledge of the structure of reality.

One can appreciate why Maimonides was so eager to emphasize the unity of the attributes of knowledge in the deity, since he argues that the attributes of God do not constitute a multiplicity and are merely aspects of the divine unity. But why does he claim that the same principles of unity apply to human beings? Why are we identical to our mind and the objects of our mind when we are thinking of the essences of things? The argument here is that when we concentrate upon formal and abstract knowledge we are no longer concerned with the contingent and transient aspects of the world. These abstract objects of knowledge constitute the most worthwhile objects of knowledge which we can apprehend, and again in Aristotelian terms we are most ourselves, we come nearest to our essence, when we concentrate upon such material. God is always concentrating upon formal principles which underlie our knowledge, and so he is perpetually in tune with his essence. We, by contrast, are frequently distracted by the everyday events of the world of generation and corruption, and the unity between knower, known, and

mind is then compromised. For example, 'the active intellect sometimes gets an impediment that hinders its act – even if this impediment does not proceed from this intellect's essence, but is extraneous
to it – being a certain motion happening to it by accident' (*GP* I,
68; 166). There are frequent impediments in our lives to our awareness of the essential aspects of the world, and for this reason there
is another form of perfection available to us as human beings, one
based upon right practice and moral worth. For God, though, there
is no impediment and he has his mind set firmly upon the really
important principles on which reality is based. Yet the principle of
knowledge is the same for us and for God, the only distinction being
that we can only really know things for part of the time, while God
knows them all the time.

This seems to be a good example of Maimonides contravening
his major principle that when we talk of divine knowledge and
human knowledge we are talking about two entirely different concepts. It is not possible to move from what we understand by our
sort of knowledge to a notion of divine knowledge which is an
analogical extension of that with which we are accustomed. Yet
here he not only says that these notions of divine and human
knowledge are related, but they are exactly the same. Is he contradicting himself? We can find an escape route for Maimonides, in
the distinction between the meaning of knowledge as applied to us
and the meaning of knowledge as applied to God. Wide as this gap
is, it still involves identifying a common notion in the sense that
we understand something different from the sentence 'God knows'
to that of 'God acts'. We should not fall into the trap of thinking
that just because we think we can talk about God knowing, we
understand the full ramifications of that linguistic usage. If we refer
back to Maimonides' example of the difference between maker's
knowledge and ordinary knowledge, we become aware that despite
the great difference in these uses of the term 'knowledge' they do
both refer to the same concept. According to Maimonides, when we
explore the meaning of human and divine knowledge, we discover a
vast gulf of meaning between them.

What is the precise nature of this gap? There exist a number of
different views on this issue. Some commentators, the most persuasive one at present being Shlomo Pines, have argued that we should
stress what Maimonides has to say about the limitations of human
knowledge. The question comes down to the amount of metaphys-

ical knowledge which we can grasp. When he talks of the distinction between different sorts of people in terms of their nearness to the ruler (here standing for the deity) he clearly has an overwhelmingly high regard for metaphysics:

> He, however, who has achieved demonstration to the extent that that is possible, of every thing that may be demonstrated; and who has ascertained in divine matters, to the extent that that is possible, everything that may be ascertained; and who has come close to certainty in those matters in which one can only come close to it – has come to be with the ruler in the inner part of the habitation.
>
> (*GP* III, 51; 619)

How far does demonstrative knowledge extend for human beings? We can apprehend the laws of the natural world 'beneath the heavens, for that is his world and his dwelling-place in which he has been placed and of which he himself is a part' (*GP* II, 24). But we do not know what laws apply to the heavens and only guesswork on our part is appropriate there. When it comes to knowledge of God and the separate intellects, all we can say is that only negative judgments are possible, and even these have to be carefully phrased. As we have seen, all we can know of the deity is the nature of his actions, and these do not give us any grounds for assertions about his essence.

Why cannot we know anything of God and his attributes? One answer which Maimonides gives is in terms of the vast distance between us and the deity. The distance seems to lie between the material and the immaterial, as Maimonides suggests in his famous claim that:

> Matter is a strong veil preventing the apprehension of what is separate from matter as it really is. It does this even if it is the noblest and purest matter . . . even if it is the matter of the heavenly spheres . . . whenever our intellect aspires to apprehend the deity or one of the intellects, there subsists this great veil interposed between the two.
>
> (*GP* III, 9; 436–7)

The difference between sublunar matter and celestial matter is not one of kind but of degree, and yet we cannot move from what we experience and understand to what lies above us. Even greater,

107

then, is the impossibility on this account for any knowledge to become conceivable of immaterial and divine things. Yet we have just seen that at *GP* I, 68 he argues that we can know that God's form of knowledge is in one crucial aspect identical to our way of knowing. Pines argues that we should not take this claim at face value, especially as Maimonides describes this account of God's knowledge as a *shuhra* which he translates as 'generally admitted', or a truth which lacks demonstrative validity. Pines suggests that Maimonides is merely reporting what philosophers call God's knowledge rather than endorsing that opinion. This account of God's knowledge may be believed, but cannot be proved to be true. Pines uses this point to argue that Maimonides was making Kantian kinds of distinctions between that which may (and indeed must) be believed on religious and practical grounds, and what we can know to be true on scientific grounds.

There is scope for this interpretation, since Maimonides does frequently contrast demonstrative with less-than-demonstrative truths. For example, he argues that Aristotle shows that the issue of the eternity of the world is not soluble demonstratively, and we can believe what we like on the matter from a philosophical view. We can know demonstratively that God exists since there are proofs of sufficient rigour to establish this conclusion, but we cannot argue demonstratively that God has certain properties. We can prove that God exists, but not how he exists, i.e. what his qualities are (*GP* I, 58). We can prove demonstratively that the four characteristics of power, life, knowledge and will are divine characteristics, but only in the sense that they are 'to be considered . . . in reference to things that are created' (*GP* I, 53; 122). We are by now familiar with some of the complications applying to divine names and their pure equivocality with reference to our ordinary names. Maimonides at every stage insisted that in the case of God there is no distinction between essence and existence, which is far from the case with the ordinary things in the world of generation and corruption. Yet even though we are restricted to referring to God through language about his actions and negative statements, we may nonetheless refer to him. Even when we say that 'He knows by a knowledge that is not like our knowledge' (*GP* I, 60; 144), we understand what it means to talk about knowledge. We can indeed distinguish his knowledge from what we regard as knowledge, and yet there must be something in common between the two notions which goes beyond the mere name if, for example, we are able to refer to divine providence in the order of the natural world as an instance of God's knowledge. It might be said that we understand that God knows but not how he knows, but even this formulation is slightly misleading. We do understand how God knows in the sense that it takes the form of a very different process than exists in our case. This is not a fact which we discover, but a result of philosophical reasoning which leads to an entirely secure conclusion since it works from necessary premises via a valid decision procedure. The attempt at interpreting Maimonides as an early Kant goes awry, although we shall see that the notion of what attitude is appropriate to knowledge and evidence in different areas of human discourse is important for Maimonides, as indeed it was for Kant. But in this as in so much else the medieval philosopher was exploring with the aid of Aristotelian machinery the conceptual world set before him by scripture and medieval philosophy.

7

How do we know?

Within the tradition of Islamic philosophy the concept of knowledge is very controversial. This is because of the specifically Aristotelian interpretation of what it is that does the knowing, the soul, and the relationship of the soul to the body. According to Aristotle, the soul is the perfection of a natural body which lives (*De Anima*, 412a 23–4) in the sense that it is the body's form or essence. The soul and body are linked together in more than a contingent manner, and the idea that the body is a mere container for the soul is firmly rejected by Aristotle. Such a doctrine leads naturally to problems with the notion of immortality, and some of the Islamic philosophers such as Avicenna tried to avoid these problems by modifying the Aristotelian thesis. One might argue with Avicenna that it is possible to combine the notion of the soul being the body's form and yet also an immortal substance (*I*, pp. 92–8). Maimonides, by contrast, adheres quite faithfully to the Aristotelian view of the soul as in some ways a physical faculty. What he means when he points to the physicality of the soul is the fact that when we talk about persons we are talking about a particular combination of form and matter which constitutes just one substance. The soul is not a separate substance inhabiting a body, but rather a part of what it means to be a human being.

Aristotle does not leave the discussion at this stage, however, but is drawn to speculate on what it is that makes thinking possible. In an obscure yet richly suggestive passage at *De Anima*, 430a 10–25 he mentions a contrast between two sorts of intellect, one which exists only potentially until it is affected by the other, which affects it rather in the way in which light affects that which is transparent.

This is a contrast between the material or possible intellect which requires the influence of an active intellect to function in the way it does. Just in the way that a body requires the influence of a soul before we can talk about human beings, so our capacity to think does not function until it is affected by a principle of thought, and that principle makes human thought possible. Aristotle seems to imply that this principle is not affected by the mutability and ultimate disintegration of the human mind, and there has been great controversy ever since his *De Anima* has been studied over the appropriate interpretation of this passage. Two commentators in particular were highly influential for the understanding of this notion by philosophers in the Islamic world: Alexander of Aphrodisias (fl. AD 205) and Themistius (c. AD 317–388). The former identified the active intellect with the deity, and argues that human beings can only have material intellects. As we refine our notions more and more we reach purer ideas which approach the conditions of intelligibility ultimately represented by God. We shall see that this approach deeply influenced Maimonides. Themistius, by contrast, insisted that it is inappropriate to identify the active intellect with God. A popular way of placing the active intellect in Islamic philosophy is as the lowest of the intelligences which act on the sublunary world and transform human potentiality for abstract thought into actual abstract thought. This seems to be the view of both Farabi and Avicenna.

By contrast, Maimonides comes much closer to the interpretation of the active intellect offered by Alexander of Aphrodisias. The latter's view of the material intellect is that it is 'only a predisposition' (*De anima*, 84 24–5) in the sense that the human mind is nothing more than the result of a particular mixture of the parts of the body. Although there are clearly differences between the ability to think rationally and the ability to eat bread, for Alexander these are both ultimately derivative from the way in which the elements of the physical organism are combined and distributed in a particular person. The ability to think, the rational faculty, represents what Maimonides counts as the form of human beings, but it is assumed that something brings this potentiality into actuality by affecting the material intellect from without the human being. This led to a problem for Alexander, since he wished to combine the thesis that the material intellect is nothing more than the result of a physical combination, and yet at the same time that it is separate from the body. In his view it is not appropriate to compare the material intellect to a thing like an uninscribed tablet (*De Anima*, 430a 1–2) but rather to the absence of writing on a tablet, which represents nothing more than a possibility unconnected with any particular thing (*De anima* 84, 24–8). He wants to distinguish between human faculties like movement which he thought we operate at a particular time just by virtue of being human beings, and the ability to think rationally, which requires exercise and training (*De anima* 81, 25–82, 5). What is it that brings our ability to think from the stage of just being an ability to being an actuality? According to Maimonides, the existence of the active intellect 'is indicated by the fact that our intellect passes from potentiality to actuality, and that the forms of existent beings subject to generation and corruption are actualized after having been only potential in matter' (*GP* II, 4; 257).

Maimonides is very careful in his use of language here. He does not talk about the causal influence of the active intellect, but just the effect of its existence bringing about the move from potentiality to actuality. To use his example in this section, a builder is a builder because he has in his mind the form of a house, which he can later actualize in physical reality by producing a house. It is the form which makes possible the later combination of form and matter in the production of the house. The active intellect symbolizes the collection of forms of things in the world, and its existence makes possible the intelligibility of those things. Knowing that p is a matter of apprehending the form of p, and this might be achieved in a number of different ways, either by abstraction of a material object's material aspects, or through constructing a concept by means of pure inference. Once we have perfected our intellect we 'know everything about all the things that it is within the capacity of people to know' (*GP* III, 27; 510). There is a great deal which falls outside this capacity, according to Maimonides, like the number of the stars and the species of living creatures, minerals and plants (*GP* I, 31). This kind of perfection results in an abstraction of the mind from the context of the material world, since there is sufficient formal material in the mind itself to form the basis of the thoughts which will then take place. There is no necessity to look outside the mind for its matter. This stage of apprehension, generally called that of the acquired intellect, is important because it produces grounds for freeing the mind from its temporal and corruptible limitations. This is because the contents of the mind are no longer propositions involving temporal and corruptible things, but rather the very abstract principles and axioms which make up those things' forms. This is not a conclusion available to Alexander with his naturalistic interpretation of the mind, but it was readily grasped by a number of Islamic philosophers, and Maimonides himself seems to make something of it.

How does the acquired intellect come about? We might naturally think in terms of something from outside of us affecting our minds in some way which results in their perfection, but this is clearly not what Maimonides has in mind. The divine intellect is said to be in conjunction with human beings, but this conjunction (*ittiṣāl*) is not to be understood as a causal relation. What this means is that there exists a collection of forms which has to be employed when we are to have formal knowledge of anything, and we might acquire such knowledge if we are properly trained, morally virtuous and energetic enough in our thinking. It is rather like going to the garden shed to collect tools which are necessary if gardening is to take place. If we know what we are doing then we know what tools we require and how to get to the shed. We do not and must not expect the shed to find us and to provide us with tools, in the way in which the sun finds us and provides us with light. To take a familiar example in the *Guide*, the prophet is a person who has perfected to the highest possible level his imaginative and intellectual thinking abilities. The description of prophecy as an 'overflow coming from God through the intermediacy of the active intellect' which affects first the rational faculty and then the imagination (*GP* II, 36) is to make a statement about the person and his upbringing and moral character, not about something happening to him. People are prophets for the same reasons that people are gardeners, because they prepare themselves adequately for the activity which they undertake to perform.

Where does this kind of approach leave the soul? We appear to have here an entirely naturalistic version of the mind, which does indeed make passing references to the active intellect and to the immortality of the source of our formal notions, yet the way in which we can think seems to be a matter of our personalities and constitutions rather than something from outside of us affecting us and raising us to superior levels of consciousness. But Maimonides does argue that something of us survives death, and he uses to make his point the nature of the subject matter of the perfected soul. Once the intellect has become perfect it can be regarded as immortal since it consists of a collection of concepts pure enough, i.e. abstracted from sense perception and imagination, to make it possible to operate without the interference of the body (*GP* III, 27). But there is a problem here. Although Aristotle does indeed refer very briefly and in a guarded way to how 'the mind, presumably, is something more divine and unaffected' (*De Anima*, 408b 19–30) by the death of the individual, the soul is the form of the individual, and with the death of the individual we cannot speak about the same form persisting. That form is the form of something which is nothing more than potentially aware of what is available to it to know, but once that potentiality has been actualized, a different thing has come into existence. And this perfected thing does not decay and die with the death of the individual person (*GP* I, 70). This has what might be thought of as rather awkward consequences for a straightforward religious view, because Maimonides is not arguing that what survives death is an individual immortal soul thinking about abstract and pure entities. What survives death are the ideas themselves, since with the decay of matter there is nothing to distinguish between one possessor of ideas and another. The perfected intellects all contain the same collection of ideas and so are identical to each other. Every step forwards in the direction of immortality is matched by a step backwards in the direction of impersonality.

8

The next world

Many aspects of Maimonides' work were attacked during his life-time and after his death, and one of the most controversial topics was felt to be his discussion (or perhaps his lack of discussion) of resurrection and the afterlife. If we follow the logic of Maimonides' view of the person and the natural world, it is difficult to see what scope there could be for physical resurrection after death. Once a human being dies and his body decays the bits which were part of his body are no longer available to be something else, e.g. a new person. They behave in a way common to all matter and change into something else. The souls of human beings, if we want to talk about such things, cannot be distinguished numerically from each other after death. The only criterion of differentiation which exists for people is material, and after death there is no way of saying whether one soul belongs (or belonged) to one particular individual or not. In the *Guide* there is very little mention of resurrection and the next world in any but an honorary sense. Maimonides does quite often refer to the next world, but it is not clear whether he regards this as a real place with inhabitants corresponding to the descriptions of the scriptures, or whether it is an idea designed to motivate people to behave in morally acceptable ways.

It is not, then, surprising that this topic which Maimonides appears to avoid in his philosophical work should be taken up by commentators and religious authorities and used to attack his approach to religion. He obviously felt he had to reply directly to this attack, and his *Treatise on Resurrection* is specifically designed to attend to this task. He claims in the *Treatise* that he will present the views he has on the topic, which he had already expressed in his other works, but obviously not sufficiently clearly for the majority of his readers. He accepts that according to religion resurrection involves the return of the soul to the body after death, and this proposition cannot be interpreted as a parable. On the other hand, he also argues that there is general agreement among people who have a relatively sophisticated grasp of the matter that our physical equipment only exists for the purpose of carrying out the actions of the soul, and given the absence of any eating, reproduction and self-preservation in the next world, there is no need to think of our life there being corporeal. He argues that the rather limited number of scriptural passages describing resurrection are far from clear and tend to describe miracles which could be seen as imaginative constructions. These passages are important because they relate to the possibility of miracles and the basis of the Law, with which Maimonides has no quarrel. They also represent for many believers the only imaginable notion of existence, since it is difficult for them to conceive of life without a body, engrossed as they are with life on the physical plane. These are the same people who also find it difficult to conceive of a deity without physical characteristics.

Maimonides makes clear his belief that resurrection is possible. We are familiar with a pattern of procreation, growth, death and decay of the body, and this particular course which nature takes is everywhere around us, yet we can if we wish believe in the miraculous alteration of this pattern. There is no reason why we should not believe a prophetic claim concerning resurrection literally, since Maimonides accepts the creation of the world in time, which is itself the foundation of all our beliefs in miracles (*GP* II, 25). If creation is possible, resurrection should also be possible. The only propositions whose possibility is ruled out of court are those which are actually impossible, such as the physicality of God, for example. Maimonides raises the interesting question in this context of why the scriptures are so reticent in talking about resurrection, in marked contrast to their frequent references to the world to come. He answers that resurrection is a miracle, and as such is incapable of demonstration. It can only be observed personally to have happened, or is accepted on the authority of someone else, preferably a prophet. Why is there a reference in the scriptures to resurrection? According to Maimonides, we can only answer this question if we think back to our origins in the society of the Sabians. This society believed in the eternity of the world and the residence of the deity in the heavens, and refused to accept prophecy, miracles and revelation. God could have miraculously transformed the minds of the people in that society, and he could thus at a stroke have shown them the truth concerning the material and abstract questions about which they were in error. But this is not how he chose to act. He preferred to act on their nature by slowly transforming it into a more receptive vehicle for the reception of the truth. That ultimate truth is that the appropriate worship of God is really carried out by meditation alone, but were people to be told that right from the beginning, they would reject it and hold fast to their idolatrous faith. So God informs us that punishment and reward will be meted out to people in the next life, and figurative language is used to make sense of that threat in the lives of ordinary believers.

In some ways it might be said that there is so little discussion about resurrection in the scriptures because people will find it difficult to believe that God could bring about such a miracle. After all:

> Man has love for, and the wish to defend, opinions to which he is habituated and in which he has been brought up and has a feeling of repulsion for opinions other than those. For this reason also man is blind to the apprehension of the true realities and inclines towards the things to which he is habituated.
>
> *(GP* I, 31; 67)

Yet there is some mention of this miracle because of the desire that God has to change our nature slowly and train us to think more of abstract and religious topics than the everyday affairs which generally engross us. We are helped to this end by thinking of a state of life after death in which something very much like us is rewarded or punished. Is it a mistake to think in this way? Well, if one follows the reasoning of the *Guide* and the *Treatise* it does seem to be something of a mistake, but a mistake with an important role to play in bringing the community gradually to the truth. The important aspect of this mistake which we must hang on to is that it has a role in helping us to avoid other mistakes. There are objections to the conception of the corporeal nature of divine rewards and punishments, yet it is an even greater error to conceive of the world existing with no moral features at all, as though it revolved around our personal interests. We can use this proposition, mistaken though

117

it is, to bring about more surely virtuous behaviour in the majority of the community.

This might seem a highly suspicious argument. If resurrection is not as a matter of fact going to take place, given what we know about the nature of corruptible matter and the individuality of the person, what justification is there for using it to persuade people of anything at all? The first point Maimonides makes, and it is a very important point, is that there is nothing impossible about resurrection; no contradiction lurks within that notion. It is quite feasible that God would resurrect bodies, albeit given the doctrine that God does nothing in vain, it is difficult to see how this possibility could be more than formal. The second point is that the doctrine of resurrection is preferable to what it tries to replace, an over-concern with this world and our personal interests in it. Even though the doctrine of resurrection describes a corporeal world after this one, it is better than the idea that nothing comes after this world, so that the entire range of valuable experiences and actions is limited to us now and throughout our lives. Even a selfish reason to look beyond our present lifestyle to something which lies outside of it is preferable to no belief in a future life. This is not necessarily because a future life will have any of the important features of our present lives. What is important about that idea is that we regard ourselves and our actions as falling within a wider context which is the basis to the notion of objectivity. The notion of resurrection has a part to play in that realization, since it posits a separate world over and against our world which constitutes a grid against which our world may be measured. Those thinkers who are more advanced can grasp this idea without any need for a figurative representation of the world to come. The majority of the community do need this sort of language to bring vividly to their minds the reality of the objectivity of morality.

It is clear that the discussion of the next life is intimately connected with the issue of providence. How does God look after his creatures and how does he reward them for their human suffering? These are issues much discussed in the tradition of Islamic and Jewish religious philosophy. In the *Guide* Maimonides takes fiercely to task the view of Razi that there is far more evil in the world than good. He distinguishes between three kinds of evil. The first kind is that which is irretrievably tied in with matter. Maimonides produces a variant of his Principle which argues that

Everything that is capable of being generated from any matter whatever, is generated in the most perfect way in which it is possible to be generated out of that specific matter; the deficiency attaining the individuals of the species corresponds to the deficiency of the particular matter of the individual.

(GP III, 12; 444)

Maimonides' Principle makes a sharp distinction between the rules which govern a particular institution and the rules of the activities which are part of the institution. Here he distinguishes between the activity of the species and the activity of the particular individuals which are members of that species. If we link his Principle with the principle of plenitude we reach the conclusion that if the particular members of a species are capable of exhibiting imperfections, then these imperfections must at some point emerge and be instantiated. Like most of the *falāsifa*, he suggests that matter incorporates the possibility of evil, and any material beings will have occasional evil events affecting them. Could it not be argued that the world would be a better place were matter not to have this effect? Could we not have the same sorts of creatures wandering about yet without the inevitable consequence for at least some of them of undeserved suffering? Maimonides argues that this would involve a very different understanding of what is involved in being a mortal creature who is part of the natural process. He refers to a saying of Galen in which the Greek physician pours scorn on the idea that we could emerge as we do 'out of menstrual blood and sperm' and not be subject to pain (*GP* III, 12; 444).

Is this any sort of answer, though? One might ask why an omnipotent deity was limited in his creation of the world to constructing human beings in such a way that they must feel pain. This question is frequently asked of religious philosophers, and there are a variety of ways of responding to it. Maimonides' response is not difficult to imagine. God could through miraculous action change the structure of nature and bring about a very different world from that which we presently inhabit, one in which pain had no place. Similarly, he could have changed our nature so that we immediately changed our practices and understanding of worship when he was intent on changing our Sabian institutions and their activities. But he preferred to work with human nature, changing it slowly over time, and permitting us to develop our characters and improve our understanding of both God and the world. When confronting the question as to why God took this roundabout path rather than the more direct route Maimonides would no doubt reply that it is just a matter of acknowledging divine choice. It is worth adding, though, that the choice of the roundabout route permits a discussion of important issues such as character, prayer and intellectual development. A deity who immediately changed us so that we became aware of all that we could know, who ensured that we avoided all evils and became perfectly developed moral characters would leave absolutely nothing for us to do except follow his instructions. Such strong paternalism would obviate the requirement that we feel responsible for our actions, and called upon to perfect ourselves throughout our lives.

Maimonides mentions two additional forms of evil. The second is that which arises through the imperfect human institutions of the state, and results in tyranny and war. The third, and by far the most important cause of evil, constitutes the evil which we inflict on ourselves. Although the world is structured in such a way that the most important aspects of our life are also the most numerous and the cheapest, through our desire for excess we seek ever-increasing quantities of wealth and fame, and in this way become involved in conflict with others, and pervert the natural ability of the world to treat us all equally. In a very amusing passage Maimonides points out that 'the more a thing is necessary for a living being, the more often it may be found and the cheaper it is. On the other hand, the less necessary it is, the less often it is found and it is very expensive' (GP III, 12; 446). He distinguishes sharply here between what we imagine we need, which results in superfluity, and what we in fact do need in order to live satisfying and useful lives. This is another example of the difference between what we know we need (through the intellect) and what we imagine we need (through the imagination). Most of the evils which affect us arise, Maimonides suggests, through the domination of the intellect by the imagination.

When he comes to discuss providence directly he distinguishes between five different views. The first is that of Epicurus, and sees everything in the world as an effect of chance. The second is the contrary view, and he attributes it to Aristotle, that divine providence is equivalent to natural law. Everything which follows a fixed law from all eternity is identified with divine providence. This implies that not only the spheres and their movements, but also the actions of the sublunar species which are governed by them, are controlled in such a way as to maintain them in existence and activity. That is:

> Everything that . . . subsisted continuously without any corruption or change of proceeding at all – as, for instance, the states of the spheres – or that observed a certain orderly course, only deviating from it in anomalous cases – as, for instance, the natural things – was said by him to subsist through governance; I mean to say that divine providence accompanied it. On the other hand, all that, according to what he saw, does not subsist continuously or adhere to a certain order – as, for instance, the circumstances of the individuals of every species of plants, animals and man – are said by him to exist by chance and not through the governance of one who governs; he means thereby that they are not accompanied by divine providence, and he also holds that it is impossible that providence should accompany these circumstances. This is consequent upon his opinion concerning the eternity of the world and the impossibility of that which exists being in any respect different from what it is.
>
> (*GP* III, 17; 466)

The third view is that of the Ash'arites, according to which the whole activity of the universe and everything within it is a manifestation of the divine will, i.e. divine providence. Even the smallest and least important event is directed by such a will, and the world can take any form whatsoever. God is not constrained by considerations of good and evil which exist independently of him.

The fourth view is that of the Mu'tazila, and argues that God directs the world with wisdom and fairness, so that any creature who undeservedly suffers in this world has to be compensated by God in the next. It is argued that only a cruel deity would punish the innocent, and the notion of justice implies that even the lowly louse and the flea will be rewarded in the next life for their sufferings in this. Then Maimonides comes to the last and fifth view:

> The fifth opinion is our opinion, I mean the opinion of our Law. I shall let you know about it what has been literally stated in the books of our prophets and is believed by the multitude of our scholars; I shall also inform you of what is believed by some of our latter-day scholars; and I shall also let you know what I

121

myself believe about this. I say then: It is a fundamental principle of the Law . . . and of all those who follow it that man has an absolute ability to act; I mean to say that in virtue of his nature, his choice, and his will, he may do everything that it is within the capacity of man to do, and this without there being created for his benefit in any way any newly developed thing . . . and that all the calamities that befall men and the good things that come to men, be it a single individual or a group, are all of them determined according to the deserts of the men concerned through equitable judgment in which there is no injustice whatever.

(GP III, 17; 469)

Yet a little later on he appears to come down much more firmly on the side of Aristotle, when he comments:

For I for one believe that in this lowly world – I mean that which is beneath the sphere of the moon – divine providence watches only over the individuals belonging to the human species and that in this species alone all the circumstances of the individuals and the good and evil that befall them are consequent upon the deserts . . . the foundering of a ship and the drowning of those who were in it and the falling-down of a roof upon those who were in the house, are due to pure chance, the fact that the people in the ship went on board and that the people in the house were sitting in it is, according to our opinion, not due to chance, but to divine will in accordance with the deserts of those people as determined in His judgments, the rule of which cannot be attained by our intellects.

(GP III, 17; 471–2)

The argument here is that divine providence is to be identified with the laws of nature as far as the heavenly spheres are concerned, but animals and leaves are not to be regarded as coming under that providence. It is only the species, not the particular individuals which fall under it, which are the concern of providence, except for the notable case of human beings, and then only some human beings. Only when we receive the divine overflow, when we are tuned into the highest level of abstract and intellectual thought, can it roughly be said that we are subject to providence. This is not an arbitrary requirement, since Maimonides regards a high level of intellectual thought as constituting the perfection of the human

122

species, so that human beings are most human when they are in that state. Providence tunes into our minds at that stage because of its overall concern for the species, as opposed to the individual.

He picks up this point again at *GP* III, 51 when he goes so far as to assert that:

> We have already explained in the chapters concerning providence that providence watches over everyone endowed with intellect proportionately to the measure of his intellect. Thus providence always watches over an individual endowed with perfect apprehension, whose intellect never ceases from being occupied with God. On the other hand, an individual endowed with perfect apprehension, whose thought sometimes for a certain time is emptied of God, is watched over by providence only during the time when he thinks of God; providence withdraws from him during the time when he is occupied with something else.
>
> (624–5)

We should appreciate here that Maimonides is referring to an impersonal form of providence. As we saw when discussing the nature of God's knowledge of the world, this is only problematically concerned with individuals. God should not be thought of as someone rather like us but with a far wider span of sight and hearing. He does not watch over us and reward and punish us in this life in accordance with our activities and moral characters. The process of intellectual overflow should be seen as akin to a natural process which just takes place continually, and it affects those minds which are suitably prepared to receive it and be perfected by it. Now, it might be thought that this is a bit harsh on the rather unintelligent but pious individual. It looks as though such a person will be carrying out his religious obligations in a simple and devout manner without the benefit of a beneficial providence looking after him. Such an interpretation would be mistaken, though. Even an uncomplicated believer is enabled, through his practice, to come as close as he can to an intellectual understanding of the source and basis of his belief. When carrying out the rituals such as prayer he is occupying his mind with important issues concerning the ultimate reality, albeit in a stereotyped and unreflective manner, and as such will be in receipt, at least partially, of the divine overflow and its accompanying providence.

What happens when someone with a perfected intellect dies? We have to appreciate here that a continuum of perfection exists, and one might be quite modestly perfected at one end, running to complete perfection at the other end, to the extent that this is possible for human beings. Maimonides suggests that those who have perfected themselves as far as possible do not regard death as a tragic end to their lives, but a gentle passing away into a realm of abstract and intellectual awareness. The idea is that once we concentrate upon abstract and essential knowledge, our minds become as abstract and essential as their contents, and death is merely the disappearance of the material body which so frequently interferes in our intellectual work:

> The result is that when a perfect man is stricken with years and approaches death, this apprehension increases very powerfully, joy over this apprehension and a great love for the object of apprehension become stronger, until the soul is separated from the body at that moment in this state of pleasure . . . After having reached this condition of enduring permanence, that intellect remains in one and the same state, the impediment that sometimes screened him off having been removed. And he will remain permanently in that state of intense pleasure, which does not belong to the genus of bodily pleasures.
>
> (*GP* III, 51; 627–8)

This is very much the official line of the *falāsifa*, that on death (or even before) contact may be made between the material intellect and the active intellect, and the thing which thinks becomes absorbed into the object of thought (*I*, pp. 87–107: *A*, pp. 82–103). This is the only type of immortality which is usually countenanced, and people whose lives have been dominated by material considerations will find themselves completely dissipated together with the material part of themselves. Concentrating upon immaterial and eternal objects of thought means that on death our minds have been occupied with material which itself does not come to an end. It is important to note, though, that what we do not have is the sort of individual immortality so prevalent in the hopes of ordinary believers. There is no way in the absence of matter that one individual intellect may be distinguished from another, and all that really survives our death are the thoughts themselves. Again, the account is entirely impersonal and even the suggestion that particular thinkers keep on thinking in the next world must be ruled out. When providence watches over us it reacts entirely to the way in which we are thinking, and reacts to the nature of the thinking rather than to the thinker. It is of no interest who is doing the thinking, only the character of the thought is important. Also, providence watching over us does not result in any specially desirable events to occur to us which are separate from the pleasure of the intellectual thoughts themselves. It is not as though such abstract thinkers would be rewarded with wealth, or health or power. The reward for their intellectual activity lies in the activity itself.

This comes out quite clearly in the discussion of Job and his troubles. The different answers and explanations of Job's predicament are identified by Maimonides with the different positions on the nature of divine providence in *GP* III, 23. The account of Job only arises because Job is not very bright:

> The most marvellous and extraordinary thing about this story is the fact that knowledge is not attributed in it to Job. He is not said to be a wise or a comprehending or an intelligent man. Only moral virtue and righteousness in action are ascribed to him. For if he had been wise, his situation would not have been obscure to him.
>
> (*GP* III, 22; 487)

Why not? Maimonides goes on to explain that:

> While he had known God only through the traditional stories and not by way of speculation, Job had imagined that the things thought to be happiness, such as health, wealth and children, are the ultimate goal. For this reason he fell into such perplexity and said such things as he did.
>
> (*GP* III, 23; 493)

Job went awry in thinking that the misfortunes which befell him were anything to do directly with God. The misfortunes which occur to us, as well as the benefits, are only events in the world that take place quite naturally. They may try to interfere with our pursuit of the final end of human beings, the intellectual awareness of God and his creation, but we can treat them with a degree of aloofness which is appropriate to their imaginary status as ends. This is not to say that what happens to our bodies, possessions and family is unimportant, but rather, that it is not so important that

125

it should be confused with what is really important, our intellectual development.

This might seem to be a rather peculiar doctrine. Are we supposed to accept with composure the troubles of this world just because we are still able to think rationally about abstract topics? For one thing, Maimonides later goes on to explain that the ability to think rationally about such topics presupposes a satisfactory level of health, wealth and general material satisfaction. His point seems to be that once again we must distinguish between what we would regard as providence and care from human beings and what we can expect from God. A kind and gracious employer or parent, for example, would be expected to behave in certain specific ways towards us, and we could even provide a list of expectations and criteria before we agree to call someone kind and helpful. In *GP* III, 24, Maimonides suggests that only a relation of complete equivocation holds between that notion of providence and care and the notion which we can apply to God. Only the name is the same; nothing else is shared in common between the two notions. It is important to point this out:

> so that you should not fall into error and seek to affirm in your imagination that His knowledge is like our knowledge or that His purpose and His providence and His governance are like our purpose and our providence and our governance. If man knows this, every misfortune will be borne lightly by him.
>
> (*GP* III, 24; 497)

Of course, if we suffer great hardships, this will probably interfere with our ability to think well and properly on important topics, but if we manage to establish some kind of mental and material equilibrium our ratiocinative powers should not be too much impaired. Once we realize that God is not like a loving father or a friend we make a good deal of progress in appreciating our relationship to him. We can achieve (a degree of) perfection in so far as through our own efforts we improve our reasoning powers and direct it in an appropriate direction. There is no point in waiting for divine intervention to take place.

This is not to suggest that divine intervention cannot take place. There is no reason to think that Maimonides could not countenance such a miraculous phenomenon. Yet it follows from the discussion he produces that such intervention is unnecessary. We should not expect a reward or a punishment for our virtuous and evil actions in the sense that we may expect such a result in our everyday lives. God is not like an angry employer or benevolent parent, prepared to react either now or in a future life to our behaviour and its moral status. The reward or punishment lies very much within this life and affects our attainment of our ultimate end as human beings. When Maimonides makes reference to a future life he is thinking in terms of the status that our abstract ideas have which differentiates them from our more immediate and material concerns. Such ideas relate to propositions which are eternally true and aspects of valid and demonstrative syllogisms that figure in the account of the structure of reality. We can think of the ideas themselves having a future life in the sense that my experience of toothache right now will not, but there will not be anything remaining of us to have the ideas about death.

It might be asked why we should care what happens to our ideas after our death if there is no us to experience them. Maimonides would take the line that we have to distinguish between the sorts of happiness which we actually enjoy in a physical and emotional sense, and the sort of happiness which accords with living as we ought to live and thinking to the degree of abstract intellection of which we are capable. This brings out a well-known ambiguity in the translation of the Aristotelian term for the end of human beings as *eudaimonia* or happiness (*I*, pp. 167–9). It is the happiness of knowing that we have lived and thought in the way appropriate to our species at the highest level possible. It is very possible that as a result we are not wealthy or healthy to the extent that we might otherwise be, but these are not the ultimate aims which we should be seeking to attain. Yet does not the intellectual nature of this ultimate aim rule out the unsophisticated but pious member of the community? It might seem that despite his steady adherence to the law he is excluded from achieving this highest level of human achievement. To a certain extent this is true, but it should be acknowledged that one of the purposes of the legal and ritual requirements is that they lift the minds of ordinary people away from their everyday concerns to a more spiritual realm of discourse. Although they may not comprehend the precise scientific and philosophical import of their religious knowledge, they nonetheless are not misled in the information with which they are provided. They merely receive in a different form what the more

127

intellectually gifted members of the community can work out for themselves and more directly.

9

Morality, law and explanation

The debate in Islamic and Jewish philosophy about the basis to ethics was a lively and interesting one. In theology the argument between the Mu'tazilites and the Ash'arites had ended in victory for the latter. The Mu'tazilites argued that a rational explanation could be found for the moral obligations which fall upon human beings, and such an explanation is comprehensible to anyone regardless of their religious background. Moral laws are given more force when they are wrapped up in theological language, of course, so that the community believes that God wants people to behave in particular ways, but his desires in this respect are driven by the necessity of the nature of moral law itself. It is because the law is right that God rewards and punishes us for obeying and contravening it. The Mu'tazilites give explanations of every item in moral and religious law in an attempt at establishing the rational basis to that code of behaviour and grounding it in something more objective than just the divine fiat. Their opponents, and especially their outstanding antagonist Ghazali, reject these attempts with vigour. They argue that there is no point in trying to ground the laws in anything but God, since he is the basis to the distinction between right and wrong. Although the debate is largely a theological as opposed to a philosophical contest, it is worth pointing out that Ghazali brings into operation very powerful philosophical arguments for believing that the Mu'tazilite enterprise goes awry. He wants to suggest in particular that if we are to hold onto the notion of a powerful and omnipresent deity we cannot have him merely going along with moral conventions which would take a certain form regardless of his presence or not. As with the Ash'arite notion of the divine basis to the apparent necessity of causality, morality cannot be taken to be an independent realm of rules and law which is merely given the nod of approval by a distant God. Rather, that set of rules only has the meaning for us which it does have because it stems from God and his wishes. Once one has followed a rule to its religious origins, one has done all that is required to establish its significance and necessity.

Where does Maimonides stand in this dispute? Many commentators argue that he stands squarely on the side of tradition as opposed to reason. This is because of his adherence to an important passage in Aristotle's *Nicomachean Ethics* (*NE*, 1094b 12–28) where it is argued that each way of speaking has its own rules and so it is an error to think that just one set of rules (i.e. rules of demonstrative reasoning) could cover all ways of speaking. The point which Aristotle is trying to make in this passage is that there are different levels of precision for different kinds of human activity. For example, if I ask a meteorologist for the weather forecast I might well expect something quite sophisticated and complex, with indications of changes in pressure, wind direction and force, and so on. It would be inappropriate to expect that sort of detail from a farmer leaning over his gate, even though he might be more accurate than the scientist. This is a case where we are talking about the same thing, the weather, but in two different ways. There are also many cases in which we talk about quite distinct kinds of things, scientific as opposed to moral problems, for instance, and we should bear in mind here that different criteria of validity apply to each kind. It would be inappropriate to judge scientific statements by using ethical standards, and vice versa. Maimonides does make distinctions which appear to go along with such a view of different levels of language. For example, he differentiates between claims which are accepted as a result of reason and those which are founded on tradition. The first two of the Ten Commandments concerning the existence and unity of God are said to be apprehensible by reason alone and do not require prophecy, but 'As for the other commandments, they belong to the class of generally accepted opinions and those adopted in virtue of tradition, not to the class of intellecta' (*GP* II, 33; 364). Whether or not Aristotle would agree with the tenor of his remarks here is debatable (for a much fuller discussion of this point see *I*, p. 152), but is not the issue. Maimonides seems to come down clearly on the side of the arationality of moral and religious laws.

This impression is only deepened in the second chapter of Part One of the *Guide*. There he discusses the nature of the punishment of Adam and Eve. Adam is taken to have achieved the true perfection of human beings in the development of his intellect, and yet he did not know that it is shameful to be naked. If issues of shamefulness are accessible to reason, then it is inconceivable that the most developed individual of his time should not be aware of it. As Maimonides argues, 'Through the intellect one distinguishes between truth and falsehood, and that was found in Adam in its perfection and integrity. Beautiful and ugly, on the other hand, belong to the things generally accepted as known, not to those cognized by intellect' (*GP* I, 2; 24). Once Adam had left the Garden of Eden he had to operate at a lower level of intellectual thought, and questions of an aesthetic and ethical nature begin to arise. At the time before the Fall he was engrossed in the contemplation of far more important issues than the ugliness involved in the exposure of his genitals; after the Fall, this is an issue which arises and which he has to contemplate.

It would be an error to think that this shows that Maimonides is convinced that reason does not enter into issues of law and morality. On the contrary, much of the third part of the *Guide* is taken up with long explanations for the rational basis of the laws and statutes imposed upon the Jewish people. As he suggests:

> all the statutes (*hukkim*) will show to all the nations that they have been given with wisdom and understanding. Now, if there is a thing for which no reason is known and that does not either procure something useful or ward off something harmful, why should anyone say of one who believes in it or practises it that he is wise and understanding and of great worth?
>
> (*GP* III, 31; 524)

Maimonides spends a great deal of time investigating the reasons for religious regulations and events. It is traditional for commentators to distinguish along with Maimonides between 'Those commandments whose utility is clear to the multitude [which] are called *mishpatim*' from 'those whose utility is not clear to the multitude, the *hukkim*' (*GP* III, 26; 507). The point of the distinction is quite clear. There are in religions a whole host of rituals and rules which have no evident purpose in that religious context except to represent the way in which its adherents are expected to behave. For example, rules in a religion which cover practices such as sacrifices relate to a particular history and region that gives them their unique flavour. The regulations concerning uncleanness, again, do vary from religion to religion, and reflect the particular circumstances in which one religion arose as compared with another. On the other hand, there are very broad rules (the *mishpatim*) which describe very general rules applicable in any society which is going to be feasible. A rule against murder, stealing, breaking contracts and so on must be expected to figure very widely in any civilized community. One might think that Maimonides would argue that the *mishpatim* were purely rational laws which anyone of reasonable intelligence would realize must apply to them and any member of a harmonious community, while the *hukkim* were inaccessible by the process of rational thought alone. Rationality could never determine, for example, that one should wash one's face three times as part of the preparation for *ṣalāt* (prayer) if one is a Muslim, nor that one sort of animal should be sacrificed rather than another if one is a Jew.

Maimonides quite clearly has in mind the controversy in *kalām* over the objectivity of religious law when he says:

> Just as there is disagreement among the men of speculation among the adherents of Law whether his works . . . are consequent upon wisdom or upon the will alone without being intended toward any end at all, there is also the same disagreement among them regarding our Laws, which he has given to us. Thus there are people who do not seek for them any cause at all, saying that all Laws are consequent upon the will alone. There are also people who say that every commandment and prohibition in these Laws is consequent upon wisdom and aims at some end, and that all Laws have causes and were given in view of some utility.
>
> (*GP* III, 26; 508–9)

He comes down decisively against the Ash'arite position and insists that we must believe in the purposiveness of the laws which we are instructed to follow. He identifies the appropriate attitude to the meaning of the laws in religion with the meaning of natural laws in this intriguing passage:

132

Marvel exceedingly at the wisdom of his commandments . . . just as you should marvel at the wisdom manifested in the things he has made . . . just as things made by him are consummately perfect, so are his commandments consummately just. However, our intellects are incapable of apprehending the perfection of everything that he has made and the justice of everything he has commanded. We only apprehend the justice of some of his commandments just as we only apprehend some of the marvels in the things he has made, in the parts of the body of animals and in the motions of the spheres. What is hidden from us in both these classes of things is much more considerable than what is manifest.

(*GP* III, 49; 605–6)

We have already seen that Maimonides argues that we are limited in our understanding of the laws which control natural phenomena, and it is interesting that he appeals to the same kind of limitation when looking at religious laws. Just as God is the ultimate cause of the natural laws, so he is the ultimate cause of the religious and moral laws, and yet it does not follow that there is any satisfactory explanation of either natural or religious events which is only given in terms of his action. There is natural lawlikeness in the world, and we can form scientific generalizations and make accurate predictions. This does not imply that God is uninvolved, but appealing to the power of God to explain everything which happens is inappropriate in most cases. Not because God does not bring everything about, but because in most cases we are concerned with more immediate and accessible causes. Exactly the same is the case with religious laws. Of course, they stem from God, but there are more immediate explanations of them which we can try to grasp.

Now, one of the reasons for Ghazali's insistence upon the divine nature of apparently causal events was the worry that any reference to causal necessity would demean the influence of God in the world. The same sort of problem can arise with social laws. If those laws are there for a certain reason, we might seek to alter them or argue about them by using that reason as a principle of alteration. Maimonides refers to the idea 'that God hid the causes for the commandments in order that they should not be held in little esteem' (*GP* III, 26; 507–8). For example, if the reason for the laws is the benefit of the community, members of the community might come to think that even greater benefit is available to them by changing the law, or doing away with it altogether. Here Maimonides makes an important distinction between the reason for having a certain kind of law and the reason for a particular instance of that kind. He argues that the institution of sacrifices has a crucial role to play in bringing about the welfare of the community, and yet 'no cause will ever be found for the fact that one particular sacrifice consists in a lamb and another in a ram and that the number of the victims should be one particular number' (*GP* III, 26; 509). Yet this claim seems to open the door to a general questioning of particular rules which seem alterable at no great expense to the institution of sacrifices itself, with the consequence that the institution itself eventually falls into disrepute and loses its power to prescribe rules of social activity.

Maimonides argues that there are good reasons for the unavailability of the reasons for some laws. We are too far separated in time and place from the original context in which those laws arose. The institution of sacrifices is devised, according to him, to counteract the idolatrous practices prevalent in former times, and the idea is gradually to change people's thinking about the nature of the deity. The practice of sacrifices does embody some undesirable anthropomorphic principles, according to Maimonides, and yet is preferable to idolatry in that it will train practitioners gradually to come to correct opinions about the nature of their faith. If we knew exactly what kinds of practices Jewish law was designed to replace in this way we should know the reasons for every jot and tittle of the law (*GP* III, 49; 612). Calling to mind yet again the comparison of religious with natural law he suggests that 'the particulars of natural acts are all well-arranged and ordered and bound up with one another, all of them being causes and effects; and that none of them is futile or frivolous or vain, being acts of perfect wisdom' (*GP* III, 25; 505). He brings in the principle of determination (*takhṣiṣ*) which was so enthusiastically grasped in the earlier discussion of the creation of the world in time to explain the particular matter of sacrificial regulations. It is worth quoting the passage at some length:

> Know that wisdom rendered it necessary – or, if you will, say that necessity occasioned – that there should be particulars for which no cause can be found; it was, as it were, impossible in

regard to the Law that there should be nothing of this class in it. In such a case the impossibility is due to the circumstances that when you ask why a lamb should be prescribed and not a ram, the same question would have to be asked if a ram had been prescribed instead of a lamb. But one particular species had necessarily to be chosen. The same holds for your asking why seven lambs and not eight had been prescribed. For a similar question would have been put if eight or ten or twenty had been prescribed. However, one particular number had necessarily to be chosen. This resembles the nature of the possible, for it is certain that one of the possibilities will come to pass. And no question should be put why one particular possibility and not another comes to pass, for a similar question would become necessary if another possibility instead of this particular one had come to pass.

(GP III, 26; 509).

This passage should not be understood to mean that there are no reasons for the laws, but that some laws are exactly as they are because of a decision which God took. We are immediately reminded of the Ash'arite notion of determination which explains the form and matter of the world through the decision of a perfectly free deity to create just this sort of world. He could easily have created another sort of world – it would have made no difference to him what shape or character the world has – but he decided to produce just this world. As far as he is concerned, it does not matter whether the sacrifice involves a lamb or a ram, or whatever number of animals that might be specified by the rules. There are difficulties in reconciling this passage with the very frequent references to the essential reasonableness of the laws, and the part they have to play in the development of human potential. The argument seems to be that we cannot at this distance from the origin of the rules appreciate the reason they take the precise form which they do take, and this does not provide us with grounds for arguing that there are no such reasons. Of course, there are cases where the precise formulation of a rule leaves a good deal of freedom in the hands of the legislator. This describes an interesting aspect of moral decision-making. If someone lends me some money and I agree to return it at a certain time and place, one might think that the rule about keeping one's promises would regulate my behaviour accordingly.

But what happens when problems arise in the interpretation of the rule, where, for instance, the creditor is not present when he is supposed to be, or where I am robbed on my way to meet him? We can think of a great many examples in which a simple answer as to the appropriate action to take is not available. We have to work out within the context of moral rules which the best alternative action would be. When one writes rules down one tries to provide as much information as one can about their interpretation under varying circumstances to provide them with sufficient flexibility to operate usefully in our changeable and unpredictable lives. When we are acting it becomes fairly obvious to us on many occasions how we should use the rules to react to changing circumstances, since we are aware immediately of those circumstances and all the details which apply to our decisions. This is partly the point which Maimonides makes when he suggests that:

> You should also understand that the status of things that are set down in writing is not the same as the status of happenings that one sees. For in happenings that one sees, there are particulars that bring about necessary consequences of great importance, which cannot be mentioned except in a prolix manner. Accordingly, when narrations concerning these happenings are considered, the individual who reflects thinks that such narrations are too long or repetitious. If, however, he had seen what is narrated, he would know the necessity of what is recounted.
>
> (*GP* III, 50; 615)

Maimonides provides what is by any account a remarkable anthropological account based upon the relative stability of human nature to explain the utility of the laws in weaning people away from idolatrous beliefs and practices. He suggests that the institution of sacrifices is a divine ruse to oppose and replace the previous aim of such practices by stealthily undermining them. He writes in some detail on how many apparently arbitrary rules in the Law have a part to play in the progress which is necessarily tardy from the primitive Sabian past of human behaviour to a future level of some sophistication. God could easily have miraculously brought about an immediate change in the mentality of his creatures, but he sought to use nature in order to change nature. He decided to allow us to change gradually from one sort of person to another by providing us with practices and beliefs which enable such a gradual transition to take place. Maimonides uses this notion of a 'Sabian' period to represent the distant past when idolatry and ignorance dominated the social and religious life of the population. There are a variety of techniques of challenging the laws and practices current among the Sabians, and the Jewish law is taken by Maimonides either to recommend the exact opposite of the Sabian practice, to perform what was prohibited, or to prevent the performance of what was an idolatrous practice. Using a medical analogy which comes naturally to him he refers to Sabian practices as 'wrong opinions, which are diseases of the human soul' and which 'are cured by their contrary found at the other extreme' (*GP* III, 46; 582). Maimonides stresses the variety of approaches taken to replace Sabian with Jewish practices, ranging from complete opposition to such practices to a gradual accommodation of the correct notion of God to the historical context within which the community finds itself. The law on sacrifices, for example, is designed to replace earlier practices based upon idolatry and the worship of a variety of deities by directing the mind towards the worship of one God. Such a law recognizes the constraints which exist in the character of human beings, however, by only trying to alter human nature gradually through using a practice which has direct parallels with the ancient practice it is seeking to displace.

This subtle analysis leads to a difficult problem. If the sacrificial rules are only necessary because of their relation to Sabian practices, why should we still follow those rules when we are far removed from those practices? Once we have discovered the purpose of the rules and we understand what they are designed to do, can we not exchange them for other rules which we might find more efficient to that end, or more pleasant to perform? The sacrificial rules might be regarded as having the same relationship to prayer as sugar does to a pill. Once a child has grown up she knows that it is important to take the pill appropriate to a particular ailment and no longer requires the sugar to make it palatable. The sugar is there to provide a satisfactory motive in the child's taking of medicine; it is not the reason for the taking of the medicine. The child changes into an adult and different levels of explanation are required to motivate her to perform actions which are to her advantage. Communities change too, and become more sophisticated and accurate in their understanding of natural and religious phenomena, and one might expect them to reject root and branch not only the idolatry of their ancestors but any sacrificial hangover from that distant and misguided time.

Maimonides does not want to draw the conclusion that different laws are appropriate in different conditions. His argument is an interesting one. He suggests that:

> it also will not be possible that the laws be dependent on changes in the circumstances of the individuals and of the times, as is the case with regard to medical treatment, which is particularized for every individual in conformity with his present temperament. On the contrary, governance of the Law ought to be absolute and universal, including everyone, even if it is suitable only for certain individuals and not suitable for others; for if it were made to fit individuals, the whole would be corrupted and you would make out of it something that varies. For this reason, matters that are primarily intended in the Law ought not to be dependent on time or place; but the decrees ought to be absolute and universal.
>
> (*GP* III, 34; 534–5)

Why? One obvious reason for the immutability of the law is its origins in the deity, and if we start changing that which is brought about by God we will be implicitly denying its divine nature. Divine laws are not like human laws which vary according to the régime and legislators in power in particular countries. Divine laws are supposed to be valid at all times and in all places, and any attempt at treating them differently is to demean them and identify them with the very different laws devised by human beings. Although Maimonides does use this sort of argument, it must be admitted that it is not a very strong one. Whatever psychological difficulties we might have in accepting changes in divine law and at the same time regarding it as divine, if we accept with Maimonides that the law is devised for our welfare then we might set about changing it to keep it in line with that general aim. We might argue that in present conditions we can change the law and make it more appropriate to the end of the law which in its traditional form embodies problematic and obscure characteristics.

Perhaps Maimonides could come back to this counter-argument with some sort of analysis based upon human nature. He might exploit the connection between human and natural law to the extent that the former like the latter can only be expected to apply to the generality of cases. The world is a perfect creation, and yet there are individual instances of innocent suffering which take place on it. God could miraculously intervene in the laws of nature to prevent, say, a child from being run over and killed by a car on the road when otherwise her death would be inevitable. On the whole, though, he does not interfere in natural processes in such a way. He is concerned with the general structure of the world, and if evil consequences follow from elements of that structure, we are not forced to admit that the structure itself is not perfect. For example, a perfect knife cannot be criticized from a moral point of view if it harms someone – its perfection is unaffected by its use. God may be taken to have laid down laws which are generally beneficial to the community as a whole and to the individuals in it, and yet it is possible for those laws to be used in ways which will not be to the general benefit. We cannot use this fact as an argument against the perfection and immutability of the laws, though, since these unfortunate consequences do not touch the issue of the perfection of the laws in themselves. They merely relate to particular instances in which the laws do not prescribe actions which turn out to be most beneficial to certain people.

Would not the laws be more perfect if they never led to actions which are unfortunate? Maimonides could argue that it is the very nature of general laws that they will have particular instances which do not correspond with the general purpose of the law. No doubt honesty is a good thing, and theft evil, yet were someone to be poor and hungry, and a sum of money was seen to drop from the purse of someone wealthy who probably does not even notice the loss of the money, then it might well be of great benefit for the poor person to keep the money and spend it on her hungry children's dinner. One might say that the general practice of honesty and the disapproval of theft are useful social institutions, and if they are to work efficiently they must be applied quite irrespective of the particular circumstances in which one finds oneself. On the other hand, the risk of self-deception is very high in any case where one tries to balance one's own benefits from breaking a rule against the benefit to the community of keeping it. After all, however deserving a particular dishonest act might be when we take account of the circumstances of the agent, it might lead to the disposition to be honest to weaken in general both in oneself and in anyone who observes the act. This is a great worry that Maimonides has concerning people who think they see the purpose of the rules which they are expected morally to follow. They might regard themselves rather as members of a club which has fixed rules designed to further the aims of the club. They might come across situations where the rules of the club go against something that they would like to do, and they might think that these particular circumstances permit such a contravention, or it might not be noticed by anyone else. This sort of reasoning process would end with the rules of the club being thought of as having nothing more than instrumental value, which indeed is appropriate to the rules of a club. But it is not appropriate for the laws which God has specified for his followers.

He gives an interesting example of someone who sees behind the laws and comes to the understanding that they are in many cases antagonistic to what the philosopher might regard as the highest forms of worship. For Maimonides, this sort of worship involves contemplation and awe, and a complete absence of the anthropomorphic implications which are intimately bound up with rituals such as prayer. He compares someone who criticizes the laws of sacrifice in previous times with someone who appears more recently and calls for an immediate and total transformation of human understanding of how people are to approach God:

> At that time this would have been similar to the appearance of a prophet in these times who, calling upon the people to worship God, would say: 'God has given you a Law forbidding you to pray to him, to fast, to call upon him for help in misfortune. Your worship should consist solely in meditation without any works at all'.

> (*GP* III, 32; 526)

There can be little doubt that the words of the contemporary prophet represent Maimonides' own beliefs concerning the value of prayer and contemplation. He treats prayer as on a par with the rules concerning sacrifices, as a way of slowly changing people's thinking about God and the nature of their place in the world and their moral obligations. The highly figurative language which runs right through the Torah and the liturgy is designed to appeal to the community at large and help it to work out how it is to behave and think in a correct manner.

This is all very well, but it still leaves the philosopher in something of a quandary, since he has reached a level of understanding of the deity which not only makes the language of prayer unnecessary but even inimical to the highest degree of understanding. The very language which is designed to attract the community as a whole is positively repugnant to the philosopher who rejects the figurative aspects of that language. The sorts of reasons which the community as a whole may have for following the religious laws cannot be the same as the philosophers', and yet it does not follow for Maimonides that the philosophers can therefore devise their own practices and rituals based upon their purer understanding of religion. The aim of the actions prescribed by the Law is that 'by all the particulars of the actions and through their repetition . . . some excellent men obtain such training that they achieve human perfection, so that they fear, and are in dread and in awe of, God' (*GP* III, 52; 630). By this Maimonides can be taken to mean that the most intelligent members of the community (in the sense in which this encompasses those best able to carry out abstract reasoning) can use the basic religious practices and rituals to help achieve the sort of awareness of the deity which they seek. They can join in the everyday religious requirements without accepting literally the language and its anthropormorphic implications which is implicit in those requirements.

How is this possible? We have to take seriously here Maimonides' Aristotelian principle that religious tradition is a process of training. He refers to 'all the practices of the worship, such as reading the Torah, prayer, and the performance of the other commandments, have only the end of training you to occupy yourself with his commandments . . . rather than with matters pertaining to this world' (*GP* III, 51; 622). This is a very important claim. Training is a process which in many ways continues throughout one's life when the aim to which it relates is complex and difficult to achieve. One should not regard the highest intellectual level of the awareness of God as an attitude one can acquire once and for all, like a degree or a medal. Religion is principally concerned with turning the attention of people away from the everyday concerns of this life to more abstract and important issues, and it is a continual struggle to achieve such a religious attitude. The affairs of this life press upon one daily, and there is a tendency to fall back into an overconcern with such affairs. A practice like prayer which is frequently performed may help in tuning our minds into religious as opposed to ordinary concerns. What Maimonides has in mind here is the way in which a person can take steps to change his nature, albeit not suddenly and finally, by gradually bringing himself to think about certain topics and desist from others. The more time one spends in prayer the less time one will be thinking about mundane matters, even though one might let one's everyday thoughts intrude upon one despite the activity of prayer. It requires constant effort to concentrate totally upon God and his works when praying, and it requires a continuing effort to change our dispositions and actions in order to make them more appropriate from a religious point of view. Even those who have achieved some success in that direction cannot rest on their laurels and abandon the practices which led them to their present level of consciousness.

This might seem to be a rather lame sort of explanation for Maimonides' point here. After all, once one had purged oneself of the need for figurative language and sacrificial rituals, why should one persist in practices which embody such language and ritual? We can take an example from the moral universe of discourse to try to illustrate Maimonides' argument. Suppose that I am very envious of the success of one of my acquaintances, and I acknowledge at the same time the wrongness of this attitude. This acknowledgement is not sufficient in itself to change my attitude. Quite the contrary, I may feel envious and guilty about my attitude without knowing how to change that attitude. The way to change that attitude involves using nature to overcome nature, to use a Maimonidean notion. I have to set up in myself the disposition not to feel envious where at present I do, and this means gradually trying to think about the other person in such a way that envy is excluded from my feelings. This process is one of changing a habit, and it is not only a rational process in the sense that it involves more than the rational understanding of the wrongness of that habit and the desirability of change. Once I have managed to change the habit I then have to be careful not to allow it to develop again. I might think after some time that I was free of the feeling of envy and need no longer take steps to think favourably about the previous object of envy, and yet given the sorts of creatures we are it is prudent to accept that there is always a danger of a relapse. This is the sort of model which Maimonides has in mind when he talks about the necessity of prayer and ritual for everyone, even those who might be able to achieve a purer knowledge of God without such practices.

They might on occasion be able to do this, but given what is known of the frailty of human character, they would be better off spiritually if they indulged in the same religious activities as their co-religionists. Both the less and the more sophisticated thinkers should use the same practices to direct themselves towards God. The former take to be literally true the figurative (and, strictly speaking, misleading) language of the Torah in their route to directing their minds away from concerns with this world and towards the deity. The wise and the philosophers use the same language but realize its limitations in attaining an understanding of the deity. They use it because they nonetheless acknowledge its value in directing their minds away from this world and towards abstract and universal concepts. Maimonides makes out a strong case for the necessity of the same law and practices to be followed by everyone in the community, and not just the less able intellectually.

If we follow this approach Maimonides' insistence upon the universality of the law becomes quite persuasive. He treats society as on a par with a natural organism which works efficiently if it is arranged harmoniously:

> Now as the nature of the human species requires that there be those differences among the individuals belonging to it and as in addition society is a necessity for this nature, it is by no means possible that his society should be perfected except – and this is necessarily so – through a ruler who gauges the actions of the individuals, perfecting that which is deficient and reducing that which is excessive, and who prescribes actions and moral habits that all of them must always practice in the same way, so that the natural diversity is hidden through the multiple points of conventional accord and so that the community becomes well ordered. Therefore I say that the Law, although it is not natural, enters into what is natural.
>
> (*GP* II, 40; 382)

The law is plainly not a natural arrangement since it is a function of society, and different societies are organized in different legal systems. Yet it must make allowances for the nature of the individuals which it seeks to regulate, albeit imperfectly when compared with medicine, which can easily be adapted to individual patients. Law cannot be directed at the individual since its purpose is the organization of groups of individuals, and it has no role to play at all in a context where there is only the individual. This is not to say that all laws are the same. According to Maimonides, there are basically two kinds of law, civil law (*nomos* in Greek/*nāmūs* in Arabic) and religious law (*sharī'a*). The former kind is directed to the best order in the political community, while the latter has an even higher purpose, to help the attainment of ultimate human perfection. Religious law is based upon the truth in a way unnecessary for civil law, since for the latter to work it is enough if it is persuasive and effective in getting the majority of the community to act in a certain way. It does not really matter whether they understand the laws completely, the motives behind them and the aim to which they point. It is hardly surprising that the Islamic tradition in political philosophy made so much of Plato's *Republic* with its discussion of ruses, stories and myths designed to influence the actions of the general public while being themselves of dubious validity other than purely instrumentally (*I*, pp. 166–81: *A*, pp. 119–43).

The Maimonidean conception of human perfection is undoubtedly intellectual. The progress along the continuum to perfection from imperfection involves correct moral behaviour, to be sure, but much more importantly it must include a progress in theoretical awareness of the world and its creator, in so far as we can know about these things. As he argues:

> In regard to the correct opinions through which the ultimate perfection may be obtained, the Law has communicated only their end and made a call to believe them in a summary way – that is, to believe in the existence of the Deity, may he be exalted, his unity, his knowledge, his power, his will, and his eternity . . . With regard to all other correct opinions concerning the whole of being – opinions that constitute the numerous kinds of all the theoretical sciences through which the opinions forming the ultimate end are validated – the Law, although it does not make a call to direct attention toward them in detail . . . does do this in a summary fashion by saying: 'To love the Lord'.
>
> (*GP* III, 28; 512)

This is supposed to allow for different means of access to perfection by different levels of the population. The ordinary believers can attain perfection to an extent because they can master the bases of the correct opinions, the ends to which the laws point, while those philosophically inclined can go a bit further and develop real understanding of some at least of the correct opinions themselves. One must bear in mind here the different routes to these correct opinions. Maimonides asserts that 'It is the doctrine of all of us – both of the multitude and of the élite – that all the laws have a cause' (*GP* III, 26; 507), but the division between the multitude and the élite comes into the open when it comes to be asked what the cause is. For the ordinary people it is enough that the law is useful and represents the will of God. For the wise this is not enough. They understand that:

> Every commandment from among the six hundred and thirteen commandments exists either with a view to communicating a correct opinion, or to putting an end to an unhealthy opinion, or to communicating a rule of justice, or to warding off an injustice, or to endowing men with a noble moral quality, or to warning them against an evil moral quality. Thus [they] are bound up with three things: opinions, moral qualities, and political civic actions.
>
> (*GP* III, 31; 524)

They have a much more complete understanding of the details of the law, which does not interfere with their faithful observation of it.

What is so wonderful about the law, according to Maimonides? We can say first of all what is not impressive about it, and that is its source. The fact that the law was established by Moses, and ultimately by God, is in no way a reason for adherence to it. As we have seen, Moses' prophecy is taken to be unique and special not because it came from Moses, but because it resulted in a unique and special law. It is perfect because it has a number of characteristics. It prescribes the mean between excesses and deficiencies in religious practices (*GP* II, 39; 417–8). This balance is taken to make it easier for believers to attain moral and speculative perfection, since they will neither be weighed down by harsh religious duties nor over-indulgent in physical activities. Then it prescribes actions which aim at human perfection in a general sense. Everyone in the community has available a set of rules and regulations which will ultimately lead to a form of perfection which is appropriate to their interests and capacities. A mark of the difference between divine laws and ordinary laws is that the latter are concerned to achieve nothing more than physical happiness and wellbeing, while the former in addition seek to broaden theoretical knowledge and understanding. This is not to doubt the significance of civil laws as playing a vital role in the development of human beings from isolated individuals to political communities in which the capacity to live a pleasant and worthwhile life becomes fulfillable. But such laws are merely the first rung on the step to the development of a society which is based upon higher considerations than just mere physical satisfaction.

It is very much the nature of law that it prescribes actions for the welfare of the whole of the community. It is designed to reduce the many differences which exist between people and to get them to acknowledge certain principles as ones worth obeying. This results in a relatively harmonious society in which it is possible for common aims and benefits to be pursued. The citizens do not really need to understand scientifically why they are supposed to obey the legal system. It is enough if they accept its main points and carry out the actions which follow from those basic principles. In some ways the divine law is subversive with respect to the civil law, since the former has as its end an other-worldly aim which has nothing to do with political aims. Yet the philosopher will only be able to work in a community which is established in a lawlike manner, since only in such a community will it be possible for the necessary physical aspects of human life to be settled satisfactorily. The religious law prescribes actions for both the ordinary believer and the philosopher, but the latter is obliged to seek further into the reasons for the rules than is the former. Indeed, the ordinary believer might feel dissatisfied with the rules if he tries to uncover their cause and does not succeed in reaching a correct opinion about them. In many ways it is better for him just to accept the bare propositions describing the laws and their purposes, and to leave the search for justification to those who are more capable of the sort of demonstrative thought which is necessary.

Maimonides' analysis of law and its relationship with moral and intellectual virtues is entirely in line with the traditional way of dealing with this topic in Islamic philosophy (*I*, pp. 166–81: *A*, pp. 132–7, 157–9). Aristotle compares and contrasts two conceptions of the good life for human beings, one which is based upon moral excellence and one which is entirely intellectual and contemplative. In a sense these two conceptions are competing, since the moral view of happiness recommends that we concentrate upon our social life, our relationships with other people and the cultivation of moral virtues and the abandonment of vices. The contemplative ideal is, as we have just mentioned, to a degree subversive of this social model, since it has as its ideal the solitary individual with his abstract thoughts and nothing else. Aristotle argues that this latter activity is more appropriate to us since it is then we come closest to the gods. There has always been a good deal of controversy over Aristotle's exact argument on the conflicting versions of the good life, but there seems little doubt that he sees the contemplative ideal as on a higher plane than the moral, in spite of the latter's status as a necessary condition of the former. This contrast between two forms of wellbeing was taken up with enthusiasm by the *falāsifa*, given the necessity which they saw existed in reconciling their views that the ultimate purpose of human life is the pursuit of intellectual knowledge with the religious conception of a valuable life as one given up for (or at least directed towards) God. They could not simply identify ordinary believers with the secondary virtues of morality and sophisticated believers with the major virtues of contemplative thought, since this would imply that God has created a world in which the vast preponderance of believers are denied the ultimate form of happiness. After all, the sorts of mental characteristics which we have could be seen as ultimately stemming from God, and it seems rather churlish of him to limit the very best form of wellbeing to a tiny number of members of the community. Some of the *falāsifa* accepted this difficulty and argued that it just is the case that only a small number of believers can really appreciate the nature of happiness (Avicenna and ibn Bajja), while others presented theories which suggested that all believers regardless of their mental capacities could participate in the best form of living, albeit from different points of view. After all, it is possible for different people to see the same thing from different angles, and it is similarly possible for people of different intelligences to approach the same God in different ways (Averroes).

There can be little doubt that Maimonides holds moral virtues to be important, but of less importance than intellectual ability. He claims that a person's

ultimate perfection . . . would consist in his knowing everything concerning all the beings that it is within the capacity of man to know in accordance with his ultimate perfection. It is clear that to this ultimate perfection there do not belong either actions or moral qualities and that it consists only of opinions toward which speculation has led and that investigation has rendered compulsory.

(*GP* III, 27; 511)

This is a topic he discusses at some length right at the end of the *Guide*. He suggests that there exists a consensus among both modern (Islamic) and ancient (Greek) philosophers, and the prophets, that there are four kinds of human perfection. These are (a) material, in that they relate to the possession of material goods such as money, land and clothes, (b) physical, relating to the health of the body, (c) moral and social, and lastly (d) theoretical and intellectual. These kinds of perfection are structured in a hierarchy, with the fourth kind represented as 'the true human perfection' and 'the ultimate end' (*GP* III, 54; 635) towards which all the other kinds point. One might wonder why intellectual thought is given such prominence by a religious thinker like Maimonides. The reasons he gives for this prominence is the self-sufficiency of the contemplative individual and the fact that he need have no contact with anyone else. The social life in which moral behaviour has a place is less perfect because it involves dependence upon others, and upon the frailty of fortune. This seems a strange doctrine for someone who spent so much of his time participating in the legislation of his community and advising on moral issues.

It is worth pointing out that Aristotle's arguments for the ultimate significance of contemplation are similarly weak. They seem to be based upon the fact that when we are involved in abstract thought we are most unlike the rest of creation and nearest to the gods. Maimonides seems to go even further than Aristotle, since the latter appears to allow for an identification between the moral and the good life, while Maimonides insists that the moral life is only a step on the route to ultimate perfection. Maimonides could present some good arguments for his thesis, though, which would go some way to making it more acceptable. Although moral behaviour is doubtless valuable, it is a fragile and threatened activity. External influences may make it harder to do one's duty, and one is forever at the beck and call of possibly confusing conflicts which seem irresolvable. To take an example, there was a controversy during Maimonides' time over the status of prayer by Jews who had been obliged to apostatize by certain Muslim rulers. Is their prayer still acceptable to God, or should they rather allow themselves to be martyred to show their devotion to God? Maimonides wrote a text on this very topic, which was obviously a very live issue at his time. The important feature of this issue here is not how it is resolved, but the difficulties involved in reaching a single determinate solution. How different such a problem is from the abstract and difficult, yet soluble, problems of mathematics, physics and (occasionally) metaphysics! Again, when one is embroiled with moral life one is forever trying to avoid making decisions which are based upon one's own interests as against those of the community at large. As we have already suggested, the danger of self-deception is very evident in all our moral reasonings, and the unfortunate situations in which we might find ourselves threaten our ability to keep a firm grip on the notion of the right action. These features of moral reasoning come out nicely in the identification of morality with a process of training, as trying to develop a set of dispositions and attitudes which are continually under threat. The contemplative ideal, by contrast, is less easy to dislodge. Once we master the theoretical sciences, we have gained a secure and valuable entrée into the realm of abstract thought, and although we might easily become distracted from that realm by the exigencies of everyday life, the particular issues under discussion are not affected by such problems. There are good arguments, then, for the very special status which Maimonides provides for the asocial contemplative ideal as opposed to the social morally virtuous life.

This argument gets us into dangerous territory, however. It would seem that the highest form of existence possible for human beings makes no reference to their specifically social and religious characteristics. The paradigm of humanity is not the solitary thinker, but the prophet, and he is a person who does not limit himself to his own intellectual development. He is intent on communicating with the people at large about that knowledge which can be formulated in such a way that it is easily digestible by the majority. Of course, there are prophets who are said to receive the divine overflow and are able to do no more than allow it to perfect their own intellects. Others receive so much that they are able to pass it on to others, making them perfect in turn (*GP* II, 37: III, 18). It will be recalled that the active intellect affects all those minds which are prepared to receive the forms of understanding from it, and this is a perfectly natural process which just operates continually. The overflow perfects the intellects of some, and both the intellects and the imaginations of others, with the result that the superior prophets are those who are able not just to know as much as can be known about God and his attributes but also can put that knowledge into attractive and persuasive language for the masses. Maimonides illustrates this process when talking about the interpretation of Jacob's dream when he refers to the climbing of the ladder as the pursuit of knowledge and the descent down the ladder as its communication to the people (*GP* I, 15; 41).

This seems rather strange, since we have just seen Maimonides insist that intellectual perfection is far superior to moral perfection, not to mention the physical and material varieties. Would it not be more perfect for someone to concern himself entirely with his own intellectual work and abandon the rest of the community to its inferior conception of human wellbeing? We have seen that Maimonides disallows perfected intellects from concerning themselves with moral questions, and have given some reasons for this view. Yet he seems also to want to argue that the most perfected intellects, prophets like Moses (and of course he thought that there could really only be one prophet like Moses), apply their minds to issues of public law and morality. To get away from this apparent dilemma we have to perform a conceptual orientation which is not achieved by most of Maimonides' commentators, and reject the dichotomy posed by the intellectual perfection v. moral perfection slogan. It is very much part of the contribution of Aristotle to philosophy that he showed how important it is to weaken the apparently enormous differences which exist between certain distinctions. We need to examine the possibility that intellectual and moral perfection might go together in particular instances of human activity, since this is clearly the model of ultimate perfection which Maimonides envisages.

How can one achieve this sort of identification between such disparate qualities? According to Maimonides, one can do two different things at the same time:

> And there may be a human individual who, through his apprehension of the true realities and his joy in what he has apprehended, achieves a state in which he talks with people and is occupied

with his bodily necessities while his intellect is wholly turned toward Him.

(*GP* III, 51; 623)

Such individuals 'performed these actions [governing people and increasing their fortune] with their limbs only, while their intellects were constantly in His presence' (*GP* III, 51; 624). He even has an explanation of how this is possible, via his theory of emanation. It will be recalled that emanation from the active intellect is responsible not just for the development of thought and prophecy, but for the forms in the sublunar world too. Even the heavenly spheres are moved by the separate intellects without any loss in perfection, since what is in question here is the provision of the forms which makes a whole variety of other activities possible. The sort of causation which is being posited here is final and formal, where the activities made possible by the cause are attracted to it and seek to follow it. The example which is commonly given here is where a loved person causes others to act in a particular way towards him as a result of this attitude of devotion. The object of love need do nothing directly which makes him such an object, yet through his being and activity others will be led to behave in particular ways. If I admire someone then my actions with regard to her may take a certain form, and that admired individual may not even know of my existence. Maimonides concludes that it is acceptable to say that the object of admiration need not diminish in her perfection as an individual just because others are drawn to her. This is even easier to accept if we examine the relationship between the active intellect and the forms in the sublunar world. The former provides the forms in our world, but does not diminish the status of the active intellect. Now the notion of emanation is frequently represented by commentators as un-Aristotelian, a Plotinian dogma uncritically accepted by Maimonides and many of the *falāsifa*. But it does capture nicely the idea that when we receive formal knowledge from another source (i.e. the active intellect) it is not like a bucket of water being emptied and made thereby less perfect. The water overflows the bucket and passes onto other areas, and the bucket is never less than full. It can both be full and fill other vessels.

This is an important idea which illustrates the reconciliation of the notion of intellectual with moral perfection. The perfected person concentrates upon the nature of God, and as a result performs morally virtuous actions. This is hardly surprising, since the only knowledge we can have of God's nature is through his actions, and in so far as these exhibit grace, love and providence the perfected intellect will seek to imitate these. It is worth pointing out here that this state will always have the status of an ideal to which we might bend our efforts. Even Moses could not maintain the high level of his prophecy once he was upset by the incident of the spies (*GP* II, 36; 372–3). One might think that this offered a good reason for trying to restrict one's relationship with other people once one had achieved a high degree of intellectual perfection. After all, we are told that even Moses, who reached the summit of such perfection was unable to maintain this level of thought due to his concern with the political events of the world of corruption and generation. It could be agreed that a greater form of perfection is present when one can not only perfect the intellect but also pass on that understanding through prophecy, yet it might be thought to be more advisable to adopt a low-risk strategy and stick to the level of intellectual perfection. Maimonides does allow for the existence of people who reach such a level and are unable to pass on their expertise to others. But he seems to imply that if one is really to attain the very heights of intellectual perfection one must pass on what one can to the rest of the community. This is not as strange as it may seem, since that level of perfection includes an intimate knowledge of God's works in the world, and these are heavily mediated by moral notions such as love, righteousness and justice. A human being cannot observe the moral character of such actions and not seek to emulate them, to whatever degree is possible.

This is the implication of Maimonides' argument, but it does not seem a very strong point. After all, I can admire the actions of an individual, and at the same time reject them as possible for me. For example, I may have achieved a certain level of intellectual awareness, and this leads me to an understanding of the beneficence existing in the organization of the natural world of which I am a part. I could agree that it would be appropriate for human beings to imitate in their actions the moral qualities which exist implicitly in our world, and excuse myself from such action. This is because I am reluctant to threaten the level of intellectual awareness which I have managed over the years to achieve. I do not wish to get involved with the upsetting and confusing events of the social world in so far as I can avoid them. This argument only remains convincing if we are intent on pulling moral and intellectual issues as far apart as possible, and then asking how we get from one to the other. The Aristotelian orientation in philosophy insists that we recognize the way in which human beings partake in both types of issues as an aspect of their nature as human beings. We cannot just observe complacently the justice of the arrangement of the universe without being affected by it. We live in society and have relationships with other people in it, and when we observe that a particular arrangement is a just one we cannot but be affected by this knowledge.

Why not? Maimonides is surely highly critical of the notion of a moral life as the ultimate perfection of human beings. Why could we not use his model as an argument for as complete as possible an alienation of the philosopher from the community into a concentration upon nothing but abstract issues? This would not be a lifestyle appropriate to the majority of the community, but one would not expect them to follow it. They should be happy in their attempts to adhere to high moral standards. When he criticizes the view of the moral life as the ultimate perfection Maimonides has in mind the following of moral laws without a solid understanding of why those laws are valid, and what place they have to play in the development of human understanding. One can adhere to laws merely through tradition, or through habit and inclination. These motives are preferable to the complete absence of any interest in morality, but they do not furnish respectable reasons for the moral activity. These reasons can only be provided by a theoretical understanding of the role of moral rules in the development of the individual from an over-concern with matters relating to this world to an awareness of the significance of the next world. We have seen how Maimonides emphasizes at some length the rationality of the law. Our observance of the law is more meritorious if we seek the reasons for the law and have an informed view of its nature and aims. If we follow the law in a sophisticated sort of way we will have to be aware of these explanatory aspects of it. It will not be enough to base our actions upon an uncritical attitude to what we are doing. Anything more must involve an intellectual analysis of our action, and so the moral life as such cannot without such analysis be regarded as the highest level of human perfection.

So Maimonides may be taken to have shown that moral behaviour in itself cannot constitute human perfection unless it is informed by an intellectual awareness of the basis to that moral behaviour. But he has yet to prove that it is not possible to stop at the level of intellectual perfection and avoid the community and the moral activity which goes along with social life. Towards the end of the *Guide* Maimonides states:

> It is clear that the perfection of man that may truly be glorified is the one acquired by him who has achieved, in a measure corresponding to his capacity, apprehension of Him, may He be exalted, and who knows His providence extending over His creatures as manifested in the act of bringing them into being and in their governance as it is. The way of life of such an individual, after he has achieved this apprehension, will always have in view loving-kindness, righteousness and judgment, through assimilation to His actions.
>
> (*GP* III, 54; 638)

One cannot observe the moral organization of the world and remain aloof from it. The sort of knowledge one acquires through intellectual enquiry is not dispassionate and objective, in the sense that one can choose to make use of it or not. Human beings have to realize that they are part of a moral order which makes claims on them. There are people who only manage to perfect their intellect in the sense that their imagination is not affected, and they are unaware of the sort of language and political skills which might be used to move the masses in the right direction. Yet they are nonetheless compelled to try to obey the moral law as far as they can, and a large part of their intellectual knowledge will relate to this obligation on them to replicate (albeit on a smaller scale) the ethical properties which characterize the divine influence on creation.

Now, it might be thought that this is all very well, but it totally ignores the many occasions upon which Maimonides states that moral terms are not objects of reason but 'generally accepted opinions' (*GP* I, 2: II, 33: III, 10). By this expression he means that they are indications of the attitude which a particular person has towards something rather than a description of the thing itself. But he does not argue that the nature of goodness and evil is merely subjective. On the contrary, he suggests that we can in principle work out how it is that we ought to behave. We ought to do our best to come to understand the universe and our place in it, since we are excluded from direct knowledge of God and his nature.

For this sort of scientific work we should maintain a balance between physical excess and deficiency in order to prepare the body adequately. We should sleep enough to be able to concentrate, but not so much as to be excessive. We should eat, drink and have sexual intercourse for only as long as necessary for health and the preservation of the community. Temperance and prudence should govern our actions, as they should govern the actions of the state, the leading principle of which should be the peaceful organization of all its diverse parts. The civil law in the state is designed to assure our wellbeing in this life and has an accordingly rather limited notion of what human happiness is. The divine law is able to make provision for not only the civil virtues of justice, peace and order but also for the religious obligations of perception and love of God. It follows that the ordinary legislator should be more than just a politician or statesman. He should be informed by an intellectual awareness of the wider ramifications of the laws he proposes to establish. Only the prophet can legislate in such a way as to satisfy both the spiritual and material needs of the community, and only he can establish moral rules which embody the mean. The perfected intellect may result in a wise person, but he may not be able to acquire the political and legislative ability to found a perfect code of law. The ruler whose imagination is perfected but not his intellect cannot extend his legislation beyond the temporal concerns of the community.

Maimonides argues that the prophet is fit to legislate since he understands the divine purpose implicit in the world. His love of God makes him try to know God, in so far as that is possible for human beings. In the last chapter of the *Guide* there is a reference to the discussion in *GP* I, 54 about the divine attributes of action. He there argues that the putative attributes of action of God should be interpreted as the structure of natural events from a human point of view. We tend to call God angry when we observe such events which are hostile to us, and merciful when they are beneficial. People will differ in their understanding of these events. The majority of the community will tend to label them uncritically with personalized labels, while the élite can see that there are natural laws which explain such phenomena. The latter will see the underlying purpose behind those events, but not in the crude interpretation provided by the majority. They will study God through the study of physics and metaphysics, unlike the masses who are unable to follow this approach. When the legislator is framing his laws he will utilize the notions which ordinary believers have of their deity to get them to accept the laws, and so he might emphasize on occasion the fear rather than the love of God, and the population will as a result not only benefit materially but also spiritually. They may pray and obey the law because they fear the consequences of offending God. This motive, although inferior to acting purely out of love for God, nonetheless directs the mind of the believer at least partially away from the temporal world and onto a higher plane. It widens the context within which his action may be assessed, and as such it points in the right direction.

In the *Guide* there is a continual tension between the views of human beings as essentially contemplative creatures and as essentially social. Since we are made in the image of God there can be taken to be some resemblance between the intellect we possess and the divine intellect. God does not need to consider questions of ethics or politics – he is entirely independent of other creatures – and there is a tendency to think of him as consisting of nothing but pure thought. Hence the contrast in Maimonides between the entirely demonstrative arguments with which we at our best are concerned, where we work from certain premises to valid conclusions, as opposed to dialectical arguments which employ for premises generally accepted opinions and whose conclusions are thus tainted by a lack of rigour. Before the Fall, Adam existed in a state of pure intellectual thought, and later he became aware of the large number of moral issues which he had to consider when he was excluded from paradise. Although Adam was at the peak of intellectual development, he stumbled through the influence of imagination and matter (*GP* I, 2). Once he became aware of his body and its needs, he could no longer concentrate upon his abstract subject matter and was obliged to set about fulfilling the material needs which then arose. As Berman puts it, 'Finally, he ended up as an irrational animal – man controlled by his passions' ('Maimonides on the fall of man', p. 12). Adam turned away from the truths of metaphysics to be persuaded by the imagination that there exists a preferable course of action than intellectual thought, and he ends up in a situation where the best he can hope for is life in a well-run state. Such a state will only cater for his material needs and will not prevent the daily struggle for existence and confusion of competing desires which is part and parcel of existence in the ordinary world. It is in such an environment that the issue of whether nakedness is shameful or not becomes a live issue. When Adam was spending all his time contemplating metaphysical truths his mind was never clouded by such fuzzy and indeterminable opinions.

It sounds as though Maimonides did think that the intellectual life is the very best end for human beings after all, and that morality is merely of instrumental value in getting there. We have already seen many passages in which he appears to say that the greatest level of human perfection is entirely intellectual. For example, after rejecting the perfection of material possessions and of physical health, he also rejects the perfection of ethical virtues:

> But this species of perfection is likewise a preparation for something else and not an end in itself. For all moral habits are concerned with what occurs between a human individual and someone else. This perfection regarding moral habits is, as it were, only the disposition to be useful to people; consequently it is an instrument for someone else. For if you suppose a human individual is alone, acting on no one, you will find that all his moral virtues are in vain and without employment and unneeded, and that they do not perfect the individual in anything; for he only needs them and they again become useful to him in regard to someone else. The fourth species is the true human perfection; it consists in the acquisition of the rational virtues – I refer to the conception of intelligibles which teach true opinions concerning the divine things. This is in true reality the ultimate end; this is what gives the individual true perfection, a perfection belonging to him alone; and it gives him permanent perdurance; through it man is man.
>
> (*GP* III, 54; 635)

It would be an error to use this and similar passages to suggest that the argument tends to show ultimate perfection as intellectual without any ethical admixture. The very best activity for human beings is the apprehension of God through his works, and as we have seen this has an important ethical dimension. This was not the case for Adam before the Fall, since the moral notions which he could observe in the creation were not principles of action *for him*, given the complete lack of a community within which to give moral principles their point. In that sense contemplation is possible without considering moral issues since it is capable of being a completely autonomous activity. Adam before the Fall is an example of the independence of the contemplative activity, but after the Fall this example can only be used to contrast with the way in which we find ourselves irremediably stuck in the morass of moral difficulties and dilemmas which characterize the social life of human beings.

This is not to admit, though, that Adam after the Fall and his descendants are deprived of the possibility of rational enquiry and contemplation. Some of the subject matter will now be of a less elevated nature, since we will have to consider the rational basis to our ethical system. Maimonides insists that it is a marked feature of Jewish law that it is in principle entirely rational, and were we to know enough about our Sabian past we would be able to fill in, as it were, all the blank spaces in the crossword puzzle whose clues for the moment elude us. We have a duty to discover the reasons for the commandments, in so far as we are equipped for this task, and our observance of the law should be carried out on the basis of our understanding of its purpose and aims, not habit, fear, or tradition.

After the Fall the difficulties in perfecting one's intellect become greater, since there are now all manner of distractions in operation, yet it does not follow that one cannot be successful in developing one's capacity for intellectual thought. The reasons for the laws are just as appropriate an object of contemplation as is anything to do with physics and metaphysics. Many commentators do not appreciate this point, taking seriously Maimonides' comments on the dialectical nature of moral issues, and to a degree they are right, since he does sharply distinguish between the realm of ethics and the realm of physical and metaphysical investigation. The former realm looks a far more likely candidate for dialectical as opposed to demonstrative reasoning which clearly is appropriate in the latter cases. We need to distinguish here between two aspects of ethics. There is the development of ourselves as ethical beings, and the rational understanding of our moral system. The former is obviously a practical activity, albeit mediated throughout by rational considerations, and it is an activity which only becomes relevant when we live in a community. But the rational analysis of our moral system, if we have one, is just as demonstrative an activity as anything else. What we have to acknowledge here is the naturalness of our moral system, on Maimonides' account. It did not arise through the haphazard meeting of custom and inclination, but on the contrary fits in closely with our natural characteristics as human beings, slow to change and requiring to be trained in the cultivation of virtues and the avoidance of vices. As we have seen, Maimonides argues throughout the third part of the *Guide* that God works in a wise and crafty way to bring about change in us slowly and assuredly, using his understanding of our nature and the sorts of experiences which will be useful to us in our role as developing creatures.

Of course, we are limited in our understanding of how the natural system of ethics works because we are far distant from the origins of the system in Sabian times, and can only conjecture concerning the reasons for some of the rules. This does not affect the assurance we are justified in feeling that those rules do have reasons, and not just some sort of explanation, but an explanation which completely justifies their role in our lives. It might be argued that this is proof that ethics and physics, say, are very different, since in the latter demonstrative discipline we are not put in the position of perplexity concerning relevant phenomena. We can observe the workings of the planets and the world beneath them. But exactly the same problems do arise for physical and metaphysical subjects. Maimonides argues that these disciplines are replete with questions which we cannot settle, given the limitations in our point of view, and although we can be assured that there is a rational explanation for the shape which particular phenomena take, and an answer to questions concerning the creation of the world in time or its eternity, we are often in the position of not knowing what that answer is. If we interpret the system of ethics as a natural system, like our system of physics, then exactly the same problems arise in both cases in coming to a determinate solution to all possible problems in the area of investigation.

What it is important to bring out here is the notion which Maimonides is trying to develop of human beings as unitary creatures, with both moral and intellectual (not to mention physical and material) qualities irretrievably interconnected within them. It is theoretically possible to conceive of someone living entirely alone and having no other object of thought than abstract metaphysical and physical issues (the point of the story about Adam). This is not possible now, since everyone lives in a community and has to think about issues which relate to life in communities, for at least some of the time. The very best state of affairs is where one both is engaged upon apprehending the intellectual notions connected to the nature of God and at the same time carrying out one's social and political obligations. This is clearly the status which Maimonides reserves for Moses and the Patriarchs (*GP* III, 51). Could we not, though, seek to rise above the constraints of our physical and political connections with the world and the community? There is after all a tradition in most religions of asceticism and solitude, and in the literature of Islamic philosophy there is the well-developed notion of the solitary thinker who reacts to the unfriendly times in which he finds himself by withdrawing into a private world of contemplation (see the discussion of ibn Bajja in *I*, pp. 178–80). Although many interpreters of Maimonides represent him as holding this up as the ideal end for human beings, it must be wrong. What we are contemplating is not just a collection of facts and theories, on his view of the apprehension of the true reality. What we are contemplating is a collection of facts and theories together with their ethical implications for the construction of our world. When we observe how God has created a particular kind of world to embody principles such as grace, love and mercy we cannot but be affected by this knowledge. Such knowledge is abstract and yet it has a very personal import for the knower. The world has an ethical meaning in just the same way that it has a physical and an metaphysical meaning, and if we are developed enough to comprehend the meaning of the world, we must be able to draw the ethical implications from what we know. The hoary old argument concerning where Maimonides stood on the reason v. morality debate as the ultimate end for human beings is misleading. He rejected that way of framing the issue in the first place, and insisted that we live in a world which is both ethical and physical, and if we reject one of these characteristics out of some misplaced theory that the other is more significant, we fail to do justice to our natural environment.

Although Maimonides insists on the relatedness of moral and scientific knowledge, he acknowledges throughout the difficulties involved in combining such different aspects of knowledge. We are led away from scientific investigation by the requirements of society and our physical needs; we are also possibly at risk of abandoning our attempts at living a moral life by the attractions of intellectual work, over-narrowly understood as just being theoretical work on abstract concepts. Even when we manage to establish something of a balance between our moral and our scientific lives, there will be a continual seesaw of instability based upon our particular concerns at particular times. Maimonides brings this out nicely in his account of the law as part of the system of training us to acquire the appropriate attitudes to this world and the next, since a period of training brings into mind the provisional status of our reaching certain goals. We may attain them, and then fall back due to lack of concentration, a change in our circumstances, an illness, and so on. As human beings we are not only limited in our understanding of the theoretical aspects of reality, but also in our practical grasp of how we ought to behave. We might decide to act in a particular way, and find it difficult to maintain our resolution. Self-deception may step in and cause us to diminish our efforts to avoid the vices and to pursue the virtues. We should use the law to set up within ourselves the correct dispositions to act virtuously and reject vicious behaviour, and there can be no conception of human life which does not involve us in this sort of conflict and potential development. That is what is meant by being a human being, having the nature of a person. We should accordingly reject any proposal to understand Maimonides as engaged in prising apart ethics and rationality.

10

Persisting problems

Why is Maimonides such an interesting thinker to readers of his work today? This might seem a facile question, since the issues we have outlined so far frequently touch upon philosophical concerns which affect us now no less than our predecessors many centuries ago. That is not to suggest that there has been no progress in philosophy, but rather that Maimonides managed to highlight in his work some crucial issues which have yet to be conclusively settled. We shall look at some of these issues shortly, but it is appropriate to point out that the reputation of Maimonides has continued to flourish while the reputation of the philosophical community of *falsafa* of which he was so much a part has almost disappeared from the philosophical curriculum. Farabi, Avicenna and Averroes are acknowledged to be considerable thinkers, and to have had a great influence upon the development of Western philosophy in the Middle Ages, and yet little significant work is undertaken today on them as philosophers by comparison with their role as important figures in the history of ideas. To a certain extent this is to be explained by the history of philosophy in the Islamic world after the death of Averroes in the twelfth century. Philosophy in the style of *falsafa*, Peripatetic philosophy, went into a rapid and apparently irreversible decline, with occasional flourishes in Persia, and was replaced by a theology heavily influenced by some of the ideas pursued by the *falāsifa* and a continuing mystical tradition which also borrowed many of the leading concepts from *falsafa*.

In the Christian world philosophy went off onto an inspiring path, practically guided by the works of the *falāsifa*, Maimonides among them (hence the references in Scholastic philosophy to

'Rabbi Moyses'). In the Jewish world philosophy also continued to flourish for a while, and several major figures such as Gersonides (1288–1344) took up the challenge represented by the thought of Averroes and Maimonides to try to make sense of the conceptual difficulties which arose in abstract thought. But even in the Jewish community where the juristic and administrative reputation of Maimonides stood so high, there existed a continual suspicion of the compatibility between Maimonides' philosophical views and religious orthodoxy. This doubt has formed very much of the framework within which his philosophical work is interpreted today, and the argument throughout this book has been critical of this framework and its implications for how we are to approach the Maimonidean corpus. If the reader has been persuaded that Maimonides must be taken to be a serious philosopher who presents complex yet open arguments to try to establish certain conclusions, then the book has succeeded.

What are the issues which remain of great interest? The most controversial aspect of Maimonides' thought continues to be his account of God's attributes. All the *falāsifa* emphasized the uniqueness of the deity and the very special way in which he has characteristics. Clearly the deity should not be thought of as having qualities in much the same way as we have qualities, and the nature of those qualities themselves also requires analysis. God should not be thought of as possessing the same list of properties as we possess, and in the same way. Were he to do so, there would be little purpose in having a notion of God – we should just be referring to a different sort of human being. Yet if the deity is a totally different kind of thing, if there is no link between him and us, it is difficult to see what we are worshipping, or how he intervenes in our affairs. This is very much the charge which Ghazali so tellingly brought against the *falāsifa*, that they had excluded God from all participation in human affairs under the guise of explaining how different his nature and activities are. Ghazali wanted to oppose this view not just because he thought it heretical (and it is worth pointing out that he poured scorn on the practice of calling heretical any belief with which one disagreed), but more importantly for our purposes here, because he argued that the philosophers went awry in their arguments.

Maimonides seems to take on board Ghazali's doubts and yet presents a theory of the divine attributes which is entirely contrary to Ghazali's purposes. Maimonides insists throughout the *Guide* that the deity must be provided with a role which makes sense of his power and authority. This role must be more than nominal. It is important to be clear on the nature of the argument here. Like Ghazali, Maimonides refuses to argue from the truth of religious premisses to the invalidity of philosophical conclusions. They both work from the basis of how a particular concept operates within a certain context, and argue that the *falāsifa* tend to drop the concept on the way to their conclusions. That is, within Islam and Judaism there are accounts of an active and decisive God, a God who is concerned and interested in mortal arrangements and who rewards and punishes as a result of his knowledge of such arrangements. This notion of a deity seems very different from the sort of God who emerges in the analyses of the *falāsifa*; they seem to operate with a deity who is hampered on every side by restrictions on his activity. He cannot be said simply to know everything that goes on in the world, to resurrect the dead, to have created the world out of nothing, to create prophets by speaking to chosen individuals, to listen to prayer or concern himself with life on earth at all. Ghazali argued that whatever else could be said for the approach of the *falāsifa*, it could not be said to embody a notion of a creator in a form acceptable to religion.

Maimonides was very much affected by this point. All the accounts of the deity and his behaviour in the Bible mention a highly interventionist individual, and it would be a misrepresentation of the text to suggest that God has the very weak and passive characteristics implicit in the arguments of the *falāsifa*. This is why he insists that we acknowledge the possibility that God creates the world out of nothing, that he can prevent people from prophesying, that he can resurrect the dead, and so on. If these notions were impossible, then there remains no room for a coherent view of an active deity carrying out such projects. The *falāsifa*, and especially Averroes, tend to argue that there is no problem in talking about God carrying out these projects. We just have to bear in mind that we are referring to his actions in an analogous way to our own, so that his actions represent the most perfect and complete notions of thinking, knowing, acting, caring, and so on against which our notions are merely a pale reflection. Yet Maimonides rejected this strategy; he regarded it as an evasion. The idea that the relationship between ordinary and religious language can be interpreted as anal-

ogous implies that we can really understand divine language in
terms of our everyday terms. However far removed those terms are
meant to be when applied to God, they nonetheless preserve some
central aspect of their meaning in their divine application from their
ordinary use. This seems to inform us of how it is that the deity
behaves, how he thinks and what his relationship with his creation
is. Maimonides is critical of the idea that we can have this sort of
information. He argues that the gap between us and God, between
ordinary and divine language, is so great that any application of
ordinary terms to the deity is a complete misunderstanding of the
significance of that gap.

Is this a reasonable view? It will be recalled that Averroes in
response to the assault on the *falāsifa* by Ghazali suggested that on
the latter's view God comes out to be something like a Superman,
someone a lot like us but much more powerful and virtuous. Averroes saw the insistence that the deity be credited with the full range
of traditional religious attributes as a downgrading of his status *vis-
à-vis* his creation. How much better it would be for the notion of
God to embody the paradigmatic use of attributes which could then
be used for finite properties by extension. We could say, then, that
God knows in a way unique to him, in a perfect and limitless
manner, and when we talk about human beings knowing we are
using an aspect of that perfect notion of knowledge which is so
totally exemplified in the person of the deity. We can then explain
traditional difficulties in understanding what it means to talk about
God's knowledge by arguing that that use of knowledge is the very
best and most perfect use, and so naturally we have difficulty
understanding exactly what is implied by it. We tend to use examples from our form of knowledge to help us understand what is
meant by God's knowledge, and those examples are of their very
nature limited to our own point of view and our own limited grasp
of the concept of knowledge and its possible range. Religious texts
are designed to help ordinary people understand the basic tenets of
their faith, and in their description of God and his attributes they
obviously have to use language which makes sense to the majority
of their readers and the followers of the religion, but this should
not mislead us into thinking that such language represents the best
way of describing God and his qualities. It provides a clue to
the real understanding of the link between religious and ordinary

language, a clue which can only be solved by those of intellectual ability and philosophical inclination.

Maimonides could not accept such an account. He would argue that it presents a view of the relationship between religious and ordinary language which brings them too close together. We might well think that once we have mastered the notion of God's knowledge, for instance, as the paradigmatic form of knowledge we then know what it is. As we have seen, he does think that God's knowledge is like our knowledge in the sense that it is knowledge, as opposed to his love or graciousness or creativity, but this tells us very little. All that we can say is that God knows, but in a way entirely different from the way in which we know. We might give some examples to try to get clearer on how that knowledge is to be distinguished from our language about knowledge, but this does not take us very far in a positive direction. It merely informs us concerning what God's knowledge is not like, as opposed to what it is like. The suggestion that God's knowledge is just the most perfect and complete form of knowledge is true, but it does not take us any way towards a better understanding of what it is. There is surely something to be said for Maimonides' analysis here. He is pointing out that the notion of the person of the deity and the human subject are so distinct that we learn nothing by pointing to comparisons between the application of the same term to them both. Averroes can be seen as having dug a grave for his argument against Ghazali's identification of God with a Superman through merely adding to the superlatives applicable to the notion of God. It is as though Averroes were arguing that Ghazali's Superman will not adequately capture the idea of God, and even more powerful attributes will have to be marshalled to do the status of the deity justice. The more superlatives we pile on, though, the more we think we can grasp a notion which is systematically elusive and unavailable to us, according to Maimonides.

Maimonides is determined to avoid the notion that God is a person like us, with a multiplicity of properties and a range of potentialities and inclinations. The interesting question which remains is whether he leaves us with enough information about God to make sense of the notion which we find in the Bible. It is all very well to argue that the anthropomorphic terms in the scriptures are figurative, and that a careful analysis of the text as a whole will point to a more appropriate line of interpretation which results in an etiolated notion of the deity, but is enough left to do justice to the God of the text? There are really two questions here. One concerns the necessity of the community as a whole to comprehend that the descriptions of the deity are to be understood figuratively. The other raises the doubt whether Maimonides leaves enough flesh on the bones, as it were (to use what would be for him a most objectionable phrase), for any appropriate concept of a God to survive. The first question is answered by him in an interestingly different way than was attempted by the Muslim *falāsifa*. They tended to argue (and Averroes is yet again a leading figure here) that the majority of the community require language describing God and his activities which is strictly speaking misleading, since they find it difficult to make sense of a deity who is to be worshipped and yet who does not participate directly in human affairs. Any Jew or Muslim would be expected to take on board the idea that God is not directly comparable to human beings, but the sort of language with which they are familiar from the scriptures does refer to God doing things, knowing, caring, threatening and so on, all of which are activities characteristic of his creatures too. Now, it is important for believers to appreciate that God is not a rather more powerful human being, and yet it is a great aid to many people's faith to think of him in terms not unrelated to those we use to describe ourselves and each other. Surely the scriptures themselves use language to help the majority of the community come to an acceptable understanding of what it is that they are to do, since most people require a message rich in illustrative material. Indeed, it will be recalled that prophets are people who are skilled in constructing such a message.

Averroes and the Muslim *falāsifa* generally argue that there is nothing wrong in different sorts of people receiving kinds of messages, provided that the messages are all true and are really just different versions of the one truth, the truth of Islam. They even go further and suggest that it is a grievous error to communicate the philosophical interpretation of difficult scriptural passages to those who are incapable of reconciling such interpretations with their understanding of religion. The idea here is that it is an error to engage in a process which will have the result of throwing into intellectual turmoil the majority of the community who are quite content with their view of religion, provided, of course, that that view is in accordance with the orthodox view of the religion. To a degree this is for prudential reasons from the philosopher's point of view, but more importantly, it is because all religions specialize in representing in as available a manner as possible difficult philosophical truths, and the whole purpose of the religion is to undertake that popularizing function. According to Averroes, one of the leading advantages of Islam is its ability to carry out that function in a better and more efficient way than competing religions. It is worth adding, too, that this theory is not based on the idea that the majority of the community are stupid, and so incapable of appreciating the philosophical analysis of the leading truths associated with their religion. Some certainly do not have the intellectual ability to understand philosophy, and must use religion as their sole means to enlightenment, but many others do have the ability but lack the inclination or the time to explore the philosophical complexities which lurk behind their naïve religious beliefs. They should not be made to feel that they therefore are only able to participate in what amounts to a pale shadow of what their religion is basically about. They have just as adequate a grasp of their faith as the philosophers, albeit from a different perspective, and the validity of that perspective must not be challenged by those who operate from a different point of view.

Maimonides' position appears to be different. He is convinced that if ordinary believers adhere to anthropomorphic notions of the deity, they go awry. He argues that all believers should put aside such notions, and adopt a purer and more accurate account of the deity about whom it is invalid to make any positive statement which delineates him in the way in which we make positive statements about subjects which fall within our experience. Of course, we can say that God exists, is a unified being and contains no multiplicity, yet this provides us with very little information. We can say that God has, in some manner not available to us, created the world and the things in it, and we can refer in negative terms to what he is not, by contrast with the positive descriptions we can give that with which we are familiar. These restrictions do not apply only to those philosophically trained, but should extend to the whole of the community. When believers use inappropriately ambitious language concerning God they do not have a different point of view of the same deity enjoyed by the philosophers. They are mistaken. But the difference between Maimonides and the rest of the *falāsifa* on this point is not as great as might immediately appear. Maimonides does contrast throughout the *Guide* a more abstract and purer understanding of the deity and the Jewish religion, an understanding available to those capable of intellectual work at a high level, and yet he too does not advocate a wholesale overturning of the ordinary and misleading conceptions of the majority of the community. We should see these conceptions as stages on the route to a developing and more accurate consciousness of the real nature of religion and its purpose. They enjoy the same status as sacrifices, prayer, belief in resurrection of the body and so on. These are rituals and beliefs which embody undesirable elements deep within their structure, and yet they point to more appropriate and correct attitudes.

This might seem to be a rather unhappy compromise between the position that such ordinary beliefs are valid, and the position that they are invalid. Maimonides seems to be arguing that they are invalid but they point in the direction of validity. His argument can be defended quite successfully. The practices and beliefs of a popular religion do more than enjoin particular activities and thinking processes. Their purpose is to get the believer to put her actions within a wider framework, within a context which is independent of her wishes and hopes. At the same time as one carries out meticulously a small ceremony of religion one is doing more than just carrying out that ceremony. The aim of the ceremony (and all the practices which are linked to it) is to raise the consciousness of the believer until she is able to grasp in some form or another the dependence which obtains between her as a person and something else far more powerful and entirely independent. This is a gradual process, since human nature changes very slowly and tends to be recalcitrant. God could, of course, miraculously bring about a change in our ways of thinking, but has chosen to act more gradually through instituting religious practices which are designed to alter our thinking processes slowly and surely, providing us with the opportunity to participate in our own spiritual development. Presumably the leading objection to God using a miracle to bring about immediate change is that it would shut off a whole range of moral decision-making on our parts which is a vital part of the challenge of human beings in a material world trying to cope with spiritual dilemmas and confusions. Were we to be suddenly transformed we could acquire no merit in undertaking the transformation ourselves, albeit with the assistance of a wily deity who provides us with the framework within which a gradual transformation can take place.

How is this development taken to work? We might start by praying to God, thinking of him as someone rather like a powerful headmaster who has power and authority over our everyday lives. We might expect to be rewarded in material terms for our prayers and adherence to the law. As with Job, though, misfortune may strike us, despite our generally virtuous behaviour. We should then question the model we have of our relationship with the deity (although we might, erroneously in Maimonides' view, also question the existence of the deity in those circumstances). This could lead us to wonder whether our view of God is accurate, and if it is possible for him to be informed of our affairs and react to that information. In coping with some of the difficulties of that anthropomorphic model we might seek to replace it with a more distant model of God, one in which he is not like a human being and is only remotely connected to the everyday events of this world. Then we might consider that performing virtuous deeds in expectation of a reward is an unworthy way to proceed, in that those actions would be far more virtuous if they were done out of a desire to do good alone. The notion that we deserve a reward for our virtue, and a punishment for our vices, would then appear to be very limiting, useful perhaps in motivating us initially to follow the law, but to be discarded once we appreciate the strength of the claims on our moral character of virtue. Good deeds could seem to be good because of their own nature, and to be observed accordingly, without any prospect of a future level of compensation. We might go on to agree with Maimonides that if we observe the order and arrangement in the world we become aware of love and grace running throughout that structure, which is not to say that we are unaware of the pain and suffering which is part and parcel of the matter of the world, and we come to the belief that God is responsible for that structure. Quite how we do not know, but that he is the cause of the structure we have no doubt. Since we are determined no longer to fall into the trap of regarding him as like a person we are careful when praying to think of him merely as a subject to be regarded with awe, the structure of the world serving as evidence of his power and intelligence. Indeed, one might contemplate at a later and higher stage of development that we would do away with prayer and just meditate on the nature of the deity and his connection with his creation, which is essentially a meditation with little or no content to it at all, given the limitations which Maimonides lays on our notions of the deity. We should be thinking about the way in which the world is organized, and contemplating the moral order which exists therein.

We have moved quite some way from the notion that the philosophical and the non-philosophical points of view are merely two sides to the same coin, two perspectives on the same object. The non-philosophical view, the approach to religion pursued by most of its adherents, is radically unsatisfactory if it remains in its present state, but since it bears within it the seeds for development into something more accurate and perceptive, it is not to be rejected. But we must be aware that we are set a moral and intellectual task by the requirements of religion, and should not relax into a pursuit of the ritual without an attempt at understanding what the ritual is for and where it is designed to take us. It is worth repeating here the well-known passage from the *Guide*:

> Know that all the practices of the worship, such as reading the Torah, prayer, and the performance of the other commandments, have only the end of training you to occupy yourself with His commandments . . . and not with that which is other than He. If, however, you pray merely by moving your lips while facing a wall, and at the same time think about your buying and selling, or if you read the Torah with your tongue while your heart is set upon the building of your habitation and does not consider what you read; and similarly in all cases in which you perform a commandment merely with your limbs, as if you were digging a hole in the ground or hewing wood in the forest, without reflecting either upon the meaning of that action, or upon Him from whom the commandment proceeds, or upon the end of the action, you should not think that you have achieved the end.
>
> (*GP* III, 51; 622)

This is not just an insistence upon the importance of directing one's mind towards God while praying and carrying out the other religious obligations. It is a demand that the believer investigates, in so far as he is able, the reasons for the regulations and the ends which they serve. Ultimately, this will come down to an awareness of the structure of the world and the divine purpose implicit within it. To achieve this level of understanding is a difficult and lengthy process, one which is continually threatened by the requirements and concerns of our daily life and the temptation to think that once we have obeyed the letter of the law we have done all that has to be done. That is why Maimonides uses the notion of training to help make sense of the idea that understanding the reasons for the laws is a process which we can undertake over a period of time, a process which is aided by adhering to the letter of the law yet which should not stop there.

Now, we have spoken thus far rather blandly about the sort of worship which ideally is appropriate, and it is a worship which consists in silent and solitary meditation, in the expectation of no rewards and punishments. Is this ideal attainable by human beings? Is the very limited conception which we are permitted of the deity capable of doing justice to the sort of God who appears in the scriptures? This has been a source of controversy to readers of Maimonides for a long time. Some commentators have suspected that he was playing the game by the rules set by the Muslim *falāsifa*, i.e. defining God in such a close way to the non-divine that his existence becomes superfluous. The argument has been that if God is as distinct from us as Maimonides suggests then he is a being to whom we can have no emotional attachment, and as such he cannot play the role of God in our religion. As we have seen when contrasting the theories of meaning of Maimonides and Averroes, the former operates with an extraordinarily radical semantic methodology according to which virtually all the traditional ways in which we refer to God are ruled out as invalid. All that we are allowed to do in the end is feel awe at the works of God, with the reservation that we must be aware that we can have no notion of how he brought those works into being. Is this enough for the view of God established in religion? A rather simple-minded answer would be to say that it was not enough, that a deity who is so distant from us is one with whom we cannot sensibly be said to have a religious attitude. Even given the fact that much of the scriptures are taken to be figurative, nonetheless we must hold onto the idea that God is someone directly concerned with us and our welfare, and intimately connected with our lives.

It is not difficult to think of the sort of response which Maimonides would make to this interesting objection. He might take the notion of love to illustrate his point. When we love someone we may initially expect to receive affection in return, and we may strongly identify the object of love with a particular individual. After a while, though, we might come to appreciate that it is possible to love without receiving anything in return, and indeed we might come to regard that form of love as purer than the more selfish variety. Similarly, we might cease to love a person but admire the effect that that person has on the world around him or her, in the sense that it is the results of those actions which make that individual a fit object of love. In the case of profane affection it would be difficult to conceive of such a case, since it is very much the individual and our knowledge of the individual which forms the basis of our affection. But in the case of the deity who is essentially unknowable except through his actions, this is no longer the case. It would be churlish to require of him that he makes himself known to us in a more direct way before we can sensibly be said to have an appropriate concept of a deity. Why should God importune us like a salesman before we acknowledge that we are confronted by the appropriate individual? The notion of God as a distant and unknowable individual is not obviously incompatible with our ordinary religious understanding of the creator. On the contrary, it is supposed on Maimonides' account to be the end result of a long process of thinking and acting which culminates in a purification of the notion of God. That notion develops from the descriptions of the deity found in the scriptures, and it sets us a project to try to complete, one at which some will be more successful than others.

One might agree that what Maimonides has in mind is a project, and a project which would take time and effort to bring off, and yet one might still wonder how attainable this project is. We are told that the ultimate aim of human existence is intellectual perfection, along with the appropriate ethical and material virtues, and that this represents an answer to problems which we might have in contemplating the end of our lives. We are supposed to think not in terms of personal immortality, but in terms of a developing consciousness of the eternal and most abstract truths which make up the structure of the world. A particularly lucid objection to Maimonides' view is to be found in Thomas Nagel's *The View from Nowhere*, in which he suggests:

> The first solution to consider is . . . to deny the claims of the subjective view, withdraw from the specifics of individual human life as much as possible, minimize the area of one's local contact

with the world and concentrate on the universal. Contemplation, meditation, withdrawal from the demands of the body and of society, abandonment of exclusive personal ties and worldly ambition . . . I cannot speak from experience, but this seems to me a high price to pay for spiritual harmony . . . I would rather lead an absurd life engaged in the particular than a seamless transcendental life immersed in the universal.

(p. 219)

What Nagel has in mind here are the range of views from the mystical tradition which contrasts the material world with an immaterial and more 'real' soul, and Maimonides certainly should not be taken to be an adherent of such mystical views. On the other hand, the general attitude which Nagel criticizes is not too distant from Maimonides' account of the ultimate aim of human life, provided that we remember his stress upon the importance of adequate social and material presuppositions of such an aim, and we might wonder how attractive Maimonides' description of the highest level of human existence really is. Job was upset by the misfortunes which beset him, and Maimonides comments that were his intelligence to be stronger he would have realized that the things he thought important – family, wealth and health – were really only useful in so far as they lead to the ultimate end of human existence, contemplation and meditation. Yet might one not think that this is a cold and disagreeable view? As I write this now looking out on my garden in which my children are arguing and playing I can certainly appreciate that my philosophical work would proceed more smoothly were I no longer to be distracted by their shouts or considerations concerning their welfare, but I might conclude that my life at the moment is a far more meaningful one with its mixture of philosophical work and other obligations than it would be were it to consist entirely of the former and not at all of the latter.

One response to this objection might be that it is just obviously wrong, in that one is taking one's intuitions based upon a form of life which turns out to be inferior, and using those intuitions to criticize a superior but harder to achieve ideal. Such a response would be inappropriate, though, since Maimonides' conception of the highest form of human existence is not uncompromisingly intellectual in a narrow sense. It is not enough for him to have people thinking in abstract terms about the structure of reality, thus ensuring their access to the realm of immortality and incorruptibility. Reality is just as much structured by moral considerations as it is by issues of physical and metaphysical truths. Of course, he does contrast the logical status of ethical and non-ethical language, and quite rightly so, but one of the most important aspects of reality which we can grasp and which we must grasp if we are to achieve a successful purview is precisely the ethical features of the natural world. Those ethical features are there to be observed, according to Maimonides, and it is one of the main aspects of reality which we must study if we are to tune in successfully to the structure of that reality. This sort of knowledge is not without its implications for our practice. It is not the case that we can observe in an objective manner, as it were, the ethical features of the world and remain unmoved by them. They call for action on our parts, action which mimics such features on a human and obviously limited scale. We have seen that for Maimonides there is no strict demarcation between moral and factual propositions in the way that that demarcation has been defended by some philosophers and many commentators. My moral responsibilities and their implications are just as much part of what I discover when I use my rationality to study the structure of the world as are the laws of physics and metaphysics.

The stereotype of the contemplative mind which Nagel so rightly criticizes (admitting that it is a stereotype) is not an accurate description of Maimonides' view. This is not to say, though, that it could not be used to attack his view that contemplation is the ultimate aim of humanity. When we consider Maimonides' comments upon the position of Job we are tempted to think that he has a rather bloodless conception of what makes life important. One's family, wealth and health do seem to be important parts of our lives, and when misfortune strikes one or all of those aspects of our lives we are rightly unhappy at the consequences. The suggestion that we should ignore such misfortunes because they do not touch the most important aspects of our lives seems very cold-blooded. Yet Maimonides is not arguing that these familiar attitudes of love for our children and concern over our material welfare are unimportant. It is just that we must put them within a particular context. We must understand that such concerns are important, but not the most important aspect of our lives. The most important aspect of our lives is to understand the role which these personal concerns have in making it possible for us to understand our place in the structure of reality. A valuable life is doubtless made up of a proportion of practical and theoretical perfection, and we only go wrong in our judgments here if we ignore the significance of the theoretical virtues. Of course, we can quite haphazardly pursue wealth, health and ethical perfection without realizing the ends to which these secondary activities are designed, and we might think that living a worthwhile life consists entirely in following these secondary ends. According to Maimonides, this would be an exercise in delusion. It would be like following a particular religious law and yet having no idea at all what the purpose of that law is, or like praying but without any notion of what the prayer concerned. The sort of moral and religious development which Maimonides had in mind could only be achieved in his terms through the influence of the intellect over the other faculties.

It is worth recalling in this context how radical Maimonides is in his separation of the realms of discourse. He argues throughout the *Guide* that the different realms of discourse must on no account be brought together, since this leads to logical absurdity and metaphysical confusion. Thinking that the intellect is like the imagination, that God is like us, that Moses is like the ordinary prophets, that the creation of the world is like the laws of nature – all these errors lead to misconceptions on our part which can have important implications for our practical decisions and theoretical understanding. Maimonides' Principle underlies the inadmissibility of confusing these different ways of speaking. When we examine the way in which the world works, we may achieve a reasonable level of ability at predicting the future and understanding the present course of nature but this does not justify us in claiming that we can understand how those laws of nature got started in the first place. Maimonides criticizes the Aristotelians for trying to extend their grasp of natural principles to areas of enquiry which admit of no such extension on our part. This leads to an inevitable problem in his account of the creation of the world, since he acknowledges the force of Aristotelian principles in analysing the laws of nature. What reason have we for thinking that the explanation for the existence of the world will not take the same form as the explanation for the existence of the events in the world, the events with which we are at present familiar? Maimonides would turn the question around, so that he could ask for the rationale behind assuming that just because the world with which we are familiar takes a particular form, that form must cover not just those specific aspects of the world but also the world as an entity itself.

One might wonder how justified he is in adopting this strategy. After all, it is undoubtedly true that we cannot became cognizant of the events leading up to the creation of the world in the same way that the events leading to the preparations of an apple pudding can be known. Yet we do commonly extrapolate from the known to the unknown, and this is indeed the principle behind our acceptance of casuality. Maimonides' doubts on this process of extrapolation can be justified, however. He is not arguing that just because we observe natural causality at work in the world, we cannot posit its operation in the celestial realm. It may be that the heavens operate along the same rules as our everyday world, but we must allow the possibility that there is a difference. Once we allow such a possibility, we make room for the notion of divine intervention in the world. Maimonides is quite clear that if we cannot talk about God creating the world in time and out of his free will, then there is no role in our religion for miracles, for the Law, or for anything which implies the influence of something from without the world upon the world. He is equally clear that we cannot be said to know that the world was created in time, but that this is an hypothesis which is slightly more probable than its contrary. We thus have a choice. We can either accept that the world was created in time, or refuse to accept this. In the first case we can then accept the description in the religion of the miracles, prophecy and so on, since they fit in closely with the notion of a purposive deity bringing about change in the material world through his free will. In the second case we can refuse to accept this form of description, and we should be obliged to interpret figuratively the stories about miracles and prophecy which we find in the scriptures. We know from Maimonides' *Guide* that he thinks that we can even derive the existence of the deity from premises which presuppose the eternity of the world, albeit on these premises we are restricted to a conclusion describing a God with just three qualities, existence, unity and incorporeality.

Is it not peculiar to base something as important as our belief in the literal truth of the scriptures on a proposition which cannot be established as true? What Maimonides is pointing to here is that if our belief in that literal truth is to be rationally based, it must be based upon a proposition which is at the very least possibly true.

One might add here that if Maimonides was an adherent of the principle of plenitude – which certainly seems to be the case – then if a state of affairs can happen, it must at some time actually happen. If God can create the world in time, then he must at some point create it in time, and this event need take place only once. (Of course, it might have not happened yet.) Unfortunately for this attempt at shoring up the argument, the principle of plenitude has very little to say for itself, and is best abandoned, and so we are left with wondering what to do with the notion of basing a whole way of life and system of beliefs upon the idea of a particular state of affairs being possible. It is rather like ordering a Rolls-Royce and a luxurious house on the basis of a bet made on the 2.30 at Chester which might possibly pay rich dividends. That would be regarded as the height of imprudence. What is there in Maimonides' account which distinguishes it from this sort of example?

Our adherence to the Law should not be compared to our buying of the Rolls-Royce, since if the bet fails the purchase fails, while if our belief in the creation of the world in time is erroneous, adherence to the Law can still continue. It must continue under a different description, to be sure, since we should then need to interpret figuratively much of the scriptures, but it could nonetheless continue. In the *Guide* Maimonides spends a great deal of time and effort explaining how a different form of interpretation of the religion would go. When he refers at the beginning to the existence of literary devices such as contradiction, ambiguity and equivocation in the scriptures he is indeed stressing the need for a religious language which is elastic enough to work under a variety of different conditions. Right throughout the book he gives example after example of how texts may be understood in a large variety of ways, some of which are entirely in opposition to each other, and this might be seen as his explanation of how religion could survive the falsity of a crucial presupposition. The important thing to realize here is that we could never tell what the truth value of the presupposition is – given Maimonides' Principle – and we are restricted to a judgment concerning its probability. Yet the issue of its truth or falsity does not really matter. If it is true, then we can adhere to a traditional version of the religion, and if it is not true, we can switch to a modified version which still manages to capture the essential features of the existing faith.

This is an interesting strategy. What is important from a philosophical point of view is that our beliefs, whatever they are, should be rationally grounded. They are rationally grounded if they are based upon states of affairs which we have reason to believe are true. If we have reason to believe that they are true, then those beliefs remain rationally grounded even if what they presuppose is false. Let me give an example here. I may finish typing and go down the stairs to make a cup of tea because I hear the clock strike four. I have reason to believe it is tea time based upon the evidence of the sound of the clock. But if someone has been fiddling about with the chimes and getting them to strike four when it is another time, my descent of the stairs is based upon false evidence, but evidence nonetheless. My decision to come down is no less rationally based for the fact that it is based upon a false proposition. This is why Maimonides stresses the possibility of creation *ex nihilo* while at the same time arguing that the question of creation is an undecidable issue. He seeks to base the religious beliefs and behaviour of the community upon a rational foundation, and the strength of those beliefs and behaviour remains unaffected by the truth or falsity of that foundation.

Suppose, then, that in fact the creation *ex nihilo* doctrine is false, and God is coeval with an eternal world. This would make it harder for many people to understand how such a God could possess the characteristics of choice, decision, power, will and so on which they tend to apply to the concept of the deity. But it would not follow that we should have to abandon religion. Maimonides argues throughout that the most important characteristics of the deity – those which basically define him logically as a deity – are easily derivable from the notion of an eternal world. Existence, unity and incorporeality form the set of basic principles in the religion, and it is possible to establish the religion on those principles. For many believers it will be difficult to understand how they are to relate to a deity so purified of any further description, but this is their problem, as it were, not the religion's problem. The important thing is that the religion should make available to such believers forms of description which they can use to make sense of their beliefs and behaviour, and any successful religion does this. It employs a vocabulary which is sufficiently fluid to allow a great variety of different interpretations of the nature of the deity, within certain limiting bounds. None of these interpretations is unreasonable if they are based upon an acceptable proposition in terms of the religion which at the time is logically connected to the interpret-ation. Maimonides regards the more purified notion of the deity as part of a project which we have to set up for ourselves and which will take time to bring into being, but there can be little doubt that for him it is the preferable alternative when considerably competing notions of God.

Maimonides is a persistently challenging and radical thinker. Basic to his thought is the gap which lies between our point of view and the point of view of the deity, between the limited perspective which we have of the world and the notion of a completely unlimited and perfect grasp of all that exists. He is thoroughly sceptical of all the attempted dissolutions of this gap by the theologians and philos-ophers, and yet at the same time the reader becomes aware of how passionately he searches for a bridge which will span the great divide. His reluctant conclusion is that we must be content to speculate as to the precise nature of what lies beyond our experi-ence, and we must limit ourselves to deriving conclusions from propositions which we can only establish as possible, not actual. Despite this limitation we can base our most important practices and beliefs upon a rational foundation, yet not necessarily a foun-dation which we can know to be true. Maimonides is quite aware of the difficulties which exist in accepting his argument from an emotional point of view. It seems that an entirely new orientation is required towards our religious, moral and intellectual duties. He does not shirk from describing the task which he sets his readers, and we should honestly examine and analyse the implications of his arguments. Whether we shall be any less perplexed as a result is perhaps another matter.

References

Alexander of Aphrodisias (1887) *De anima*, I. Bruns (ed.) *Supplementum Aristotelicum*, II, Berlin:

Aristotle (1984) *The Complete Works of Aristotle: the Revised Oxford Translation* I and II, Princeton: Princeton University Press.

Averroes (ibn Rushd) (1961) 'Faṣl al-maqāl [Decisive treatise on the harmony of religion and philosophy]', trans. G. Hourani in *Averroes on the Harmony of Religion and Philosophy*, London:Luzac (reprinted 1967 and 1976).

— (1969) 'Middle Commentary', trans. H. Davidson in *Middle Commentary on Porphyry's Isagoge and on Aristotle's Categoriae*, Cambridge, Mass.: Medieval Academy of America.

Berman, L. (1974) 'Maimonides, the disciple of Alfarabi', *Israel Oriental Studies* 4: 154–78.

— (1980) 'Maimonides on the fall of man', *Association for Jewish Studies Review*, 5:1–15.

Ghazali (1980) 'Al-Munqidh min al-Ḍalāl [The deliverer from error]', trans. R. McCarthy in *Freedom and Fulfillment*, Boston, Mass.: Twayne.

Maimonides (1966) 'Maimonides' Arabic *Treatise on Logic*', ed. I. Efros in *Proceedings of the American Academy for Jewish Research* 34 (1966), supplementing an earlier edition, 8 (1938).

— (1952) *Maimonides' Treatise on Resurrection*, ed. J. Finkel, New York: American Academy for Jewish Research.

Merleau-Ponty, M. (1962) *Phenomenology of Perception*, London: Routledge & Kegan Paul.

Munk, S. (1855–66) *Le guide des égarés* (Arabic text *Dalālat al-ḥa' irīn*), ed. and trans S. Munk, Paris: A. Franck.

Nagel, T. (1986) *The View from Nowhere*, New York: Oxford University Press.

Reines, A. (1970) *Maimonides and Abrabanel on Prophecy*, Cincinnati: Hebrew Union College of America.

— (1986) 'Maimonides' true belief concerning God', in S. Pines and Y. Yovel (eds) *Maimonides and Philosophy*, Dordrecht: Nijhoff, 24–35.

Strauss, L. (1963) 'How to begin to study the *Guide of the Perplexed*', Preface to the *Guide* trans. S. Pines, Chicago: University of Chicago Press.

Teicher, J. (1942) 'Christian theology and the Jewish opposition to Maimonides', *Journal of Theological Studies* 43: 68–76.

Wittgenstein, L. (1967) *Zettel* ed. G. Anscombe and G. von Wright, trans. Anscombe, Oxford: Blackwell.

Wolfson, H. (1935) 'Maimonides on the internal senses', *Jewish Quarterly Review* 51: 441–67.

Select Bibliography

Altmann, A. (1972) 'Maimonides' "four perfections" ', *Israel Oriental Studies* 2: 15–24.

—(1978) 'Maimonides and Aquinas: Natural or divine prophecy', *Association for Jewish Studies Review* 3: 1–19.

—(1985) 'Maimonides on the intellect and the scope of metaphysics', in *Von der mittelalterlichen zur modernen Aufklärung*, Tübingen: J. C. B. Mohr, 60–129.

Bland, K. (1982) 'Moses and the Law according to Maimonides', in J. Rheniharz (ed.) *Mystics, Philosophers and Politicians: Essays in Jewish Intellectual History in Honour of Alexander Altmann*, North Carolina: Duke University Press, 49–66.

Davidson, H. (1963) 'Maimonides' *Shemonah Peraqim* and Alfarabi's *Fuṣūl al-Madanī*', *Proceedings of the American Academy for Jewish Research* 31: 33–51.

—(1968) 'Arguments from the concept of particularization in Arabic philosophy', *Philosophy East and West* 18: 299–314.

—(1979) 'Maimonides' secret position on creation', in I. Twersky (ed.) *Studies in Medieval Jewish History and Literature* I, Cambridge, Mass.: Harvard University Press, 16–40.

Fakhry, M. (1953) 'The antinomy of the eternity of the world in Averroes, Maimonides, and Aquinas', *Muséon* 68: 139–55.

Faur, J. (1967) 'La doctrina de la ley natural', *Sefarad* 27: 239–68.

Fox, M. (1972) 'Maimonides and Aquinas on natural law', *Diné Yisrael* 3: V-XXXVI.

Franck, I. (1985) 'Maimonides and Aquinas on man's knowledge of God: a twentieth century perspective', *Review of Metaphysics* 38: 591–615.

Frank, D. (1985) 'The end of the Guide: Maimonides on the best life for man', *Judaism* 34: 485–95.

Funkenstein A., (1970) 'Gesetz und Geschichte; zur historisierenden Hermeneutik bei Moses Maimonides und Thomas von Aquin', *Viator* 1: 147–78.

—(1977) 'Maimonides: political theory and realistic messianism', *Miscellanea Mediaevalia* 11: 81–103.

Galston, M. (1978) 'Philosopher-king v. prophet', *Israel Oriental Studies* 8: 204–8.
— (1978) 'The purpose of the law according to Maimonides', *Jewish Quarterly Review* 69: 27–51.
Goodman, L. (1980) 'Maimonides' philosophy of law', *Jewish Law Annual* I: 72–107.
Hartman, D. (1976) *Maimonides: Torah and Philosophic Quest*, Philadelphia: Jewish Publication Society of America.
Harvey, W. (1981) 'A third approach to Maimonides' cosmogony-prophetology puzzle', *Harvard Theological Review* 74: 287–301.
Hyman, A. (1986) 'Maimonides on causality', in S. Pines and Y. Yovel (eds) *Maimonides and Philosophy*, Dordrecht: Nijhoff, 151–72.
Ivry, A. (1982) 'Maimonides on possibility' in J. Rheinharz (ed.) *Mystics, Philosophers and Politicians: Essays in Jewish Intellectual History in Honour of Alexander Altman*, North Carolina: Duke University Press, 67–84.
— (1986) 'Islamic and Greek influences on Maimonides' philosophy', in S. Pines and Y. Yovel (eds) *Maimonides and Philosophy*, Dordrecht: Nijhoff, 139–56.
Kaplan, L. (1977) 'Maimonides on the miraculous element in prophecy', *Harvard Theological Review* 70: 233–56.
Kellner, M. (1977) 'Maimonides and Gersonides on Mosaic prophecy', *Speculum* 52: 62–79.
— 1982 'Maimonides' thirteen principles and the structure of the "Guide of the Perplexed"', *Journal of the History of Philosophy* 20: 76–84.
Kirschner, R. (1981) 'Maimonides' fiction of resurrection, *Hebrew Union College Annual* 52: 163–93.
Leaman, O. (1980) 'Does the interpretation of Islamic philosophy rest on a mistake?', *International Journal of Mid Eastern Studies* 7: 525–38.
— (1987) 'Maimonides and natural law', *Jewish Law Annual* 6: 78–93.
Lerner, R. (1983) 'Maimonides' "Treatise on Resurrection"', *History of Religions* 23: 140–55.
Pines, S. (1968) 'Spinoza's *Tractatus*, Maimonides and Kant', *Scripta Hierosolymitana* 6: 3–54.
— (1970) 'Ibn Khaldun and Maimonides', *Studia Islamica* 32: 265–74.
— (1979) 'The limitations of human knowledge according to Al-Farabi, ibn Bajja and Maimonides', in I. Twersky (ed.) *Studies in Medieval Jewish History and Literature*, Cambridge, Mass.: Harvard University Press.
— (1981) 'Les limites de la métaphysique selon Al-Farabi, ibn Bajja et Maïmonide; sources et antithèses de ces doctrines chez Alexandre d'Aphrodise et chez Themistius', *Miscellanea Mediaevalia* 13: 211–25.
— (1986) 'The philosophical purport of Maimonides' Halachic works and the purport of *The Guide of the Perplexed*' in S. Pines and Y. Yovel (eds) *Maimonides and Philosophy*, Dordrecht: Nijhoff, 1–14.
Reines, A. (1969–70) 'Maimononides' concept of Mosaic prophecy,' *Hebrew Union College Annual*: 40–41, 325–61.
— (1972) 'Maimonides' concepts of providence and theodicy', *Hebrew Union College Annual* 43: 169–206.

—(1974) 'Maimonides' concepts of miracles', *Hebrew Union College Annual* 45: 243–85.

Rosenthal, E. (1960) *Griechisches Erbe in der Jüdischen Religionsphilosophie des Mittelalters*, Stuttgart: Kohlhammer.

—(1971) 'Maimonides' conception of state and society', *Studia Semitica* I, Cambridge: Cambridge University Press, 275–88.

—(1966) 'Torah and Nomos in medieval Jewish philosophy', in R. Loewe (ed.) *Studies in Rationalism, Judaism and Universalism*, London: Routledge, 215–31.

—(1974) 'The notion of revelation in medieval Judaism', *S. Bonaventura* 4 Theologica, Rome: Grottaferrata.

Roth, L. (1924) *Spinoza, Descartes and Maimonides*, Oxford: Oxford University Press.

—(1948) *The Guide for the Perplexed*, London: Hutchinson.

Said, E. (1978) *Orientalism*, London: Routledge Kegan and Paul.

Schofield, M. (1978) 'Aristotle on the imagination', in G. Lloyd & G. Owen (ed.) *Aristotle on the mind and senses*, Cambridge: Cambridge University Press, 99–139.

Schwarzchild, S. (1962) 'Do Noachites have to believe in revelation?', *Jewish Quarterly Review* 52: 297–308; 53: 30–65.

—(1978) 'Moral radicalism and "middlingness" in the ethics of Maimonides', *Studies in Medieval Culture* 11: 65–94.

Sirat, C. (1985) *A history of Jewish philosophy in the Middle Ages*, Cambridge: Cambridge University Press.

Stern, J. 'The idea of a *Hoq* in Maimonides' explanation of the Law', in S. Pines and Y. Yovel (eds.) *Maimonides and Philosophy*, Dordrecht: Nijhoff, 92–130.

Strauss, L. (1935) *Philosophie und Gesetz*, Berlin:

—(1936) 'Quelques remarques sur la science politique de Maimonide et de Farabi', *Révue des études juives* 100: 1–37.

—(1952) 'The literary character of the *Guide of the Perplexed*' in his *Persecution and the Art of Writing*, Glencoe, Ill.: Free Press, 38–94.

—(1959) 'Maimonides' statement on political science', in his *What is Political Philosophy?*, New York: Free Press, 155–69.

—(1967) 'Notes on Maimonides' Book of Knowledge' in E. Urbach (ed.) *Studies in Mysticism and Religion Presented to G. Scholem*, Jerusalem: Magnes Press, 269–83.

Touati, C. (1979) 'Les deux théories de Maïmonide sur la providence', in S. Stein and R. Loewe (eds) *Studies in Jewish Religious and Intellectual History*, Alabama: University of Alabama Press, 331–43.

Twersky, I. (1980) *Introduction to the Code of Maimonides (Mishneh Torah)*, New Haven: Yale University Press.

Vajda, G. (1966) 'La pensée religieuse de Moïse Maïmonide: unité ou dualité?', *Cahiers de Civilization Médiévale* 9: 29–49.

Wolfson, H. (1973) 'Maimonides on the internal senses', in his *Studies in the History of Philosophy and Religion* I, Cambridge, Mass.: Harvard University Press, 344–70.

—(1973) 'The amphibolous terms in Aristotle, Arabic philosophy and Maimonides', ibid., 455–77.
—(1973) 'Note on Maimonides' classification of the sciences', ibid., 551–60.
—(1976) *The philosophy of the Kalām*, Cambridge, Mass.: Harvard University Press, see p. 210.
—(1977) 'The Aristotelian predicables and Maimonides' division of attributes', in his *Studies in the History of Philosophy and Religion* II, Cambridge, Mass.: Harvard University Press, 195–230.
—(1977) 'Maimonides on negative attributes', ibid., 195–230.
—(1977) 'Maimonides on the unity and incorporeality of God', ibid., 433–57.

ADDITIONAL BIBLIOGRAPHY

Useful lists of references and articles are available in the following collections:
Brinner, W. and Ricks, S. (eds) (1986) *Studies in Islamic and Judaic traditions*, Brown Judaic Studies 110, Atlanta, Georgia: Scholars Press.
Buijs, J. (ed.) (1988) *Maimonides: a collection of critical essays*, Indiana: University of Notre Dame Press.
Dienstag, J. (ed.) (1975) *Studies in Maimonides and St Thomas*, New York: KTAV.
Goodman, L. (trans.) (1976) *Rambam: Readings in the philosophy of Moses Maimonides*, with introduction and commentary by L. Goodman, New York: Viking.
Link-Salinger, R. (ed.) (1987) *A straight path: studies in medieval philosophy and culture. Essays in honour of Arthur Hyman*, Washington: Catholic University of America.
Weiss, R. and Butterworth, C. (eds.) (1975) *Ethical writings of Maimonides*, New York: New York Unversity Press.
Twersky, I. (ed.) (1972) *A Maimonides Reader*, New York: Behrman House.

INDEX

Sabians, society of 116–17, 119, 136–7, 158
sacrifice 63, 134, 136, 137, 140, 169; animal 37
Schofield, Malcolm, on dreams and imagination 48
scripture, literal truth of 39
senses, and imagination 43
Shi'ites, and esoteric tradition 3
Socrates 2, 33
Sodom and Gomorrah 50, 51
soul 110, 114; as 'common sense' 45
Strauss, Leo 7; on doctrine of attributes 34–5
Summa Theologica 7

Tahāfut al-falāsifa (Ghazali) 101
Themistius (c AD 317–88), on the intellect 111
theologians *see mutakallimūn*
theology, problems of 85
thought-experiment 90, 92

thought/thinking 111, 125; Aristotle on 104–5; and imagination 50–1; modes of 86
Torah 140
training: importance of 141–2; notion of 172
Treatise on Resurrection 115–16
truth: and Islam 167–8; literal 177; ultimate 117

universe, disorder in 98

View from Nowhere, The (Nagel), quoted 173–4

Wittgenstein, L. 42
Wolfson, H., on imagination 40
world: creation of 56, 58, 176–7, Aristotelian view on 66–7, in time 82–3, 87, 88, various views on 53–4, 57, 65; eternity of 97–8; how it works 90–1, 93; meanings of 160
worship 171, 172; practices of 36